Born and raised on the Isle of Wight, Leslie enjoyed a happy and healthy childhood by the sea. After leaving school he began work in Bournemouth and later worked for a time in Paris. The years passed by, and life settled into a contented routine until one day, in the space of a few moments, everything changed forever.

Leslie Moul

God and Chips

AUSTIN MACAULEY PUBLISHERS
LONDON · CAMBRIDGE · NEW YORK · SHARJAH

Copyright © Leslie Moul 2024

The right of Leslie Moul to be identified as author of this work has been asserted by the author in accordance with sections 77 and 78 of the Copyright, Designs and Patents Act 1988.

All rights reserved. No part of this publication may be reproduced, stored in a retrieval system, or transmitted in any form or by any means, electronic, mechanical, photocopying, recording, or otherwise, without the prior permission of the publishers.

Any person who commits any unauthorised act in relation to this publication may be liable to criminal prosecution and civil claims for damages.

All of the events in this memoir are true to the best of author's memory. The views expressed in this memoir are solely those of the author.

A CIP catalogue record for this title is available from the British Library.

ISBN 9781035863488(Paperback)
ISBN 9781035863495 (ePub e-book)

www.austinmacauley.com

First Published 2024
Austin Macauley Publishers Ltd®
1 Canada Square
Canary Wharf
London
E14 5AA

My thanks to:

Andy Fyffe and Joel Whittaker, the excellent paramedics for bringing me back to life the first time.

Doctor Saleed Talwar and the cardiac team at Bournemouth Hospital for restoring my life the second time.

Keith Pollard, the most loyal friend anyone could wish to have without whose constant support during my lengthy recovery, this book would never have been written.

My goddaughter, Francesca Simpson, whose patience and speed in typing made life so much easier with my constant additions to the text!

Also, my dear friend, Lisa Milton who, like my goddaughter spent endless hours typing up and re-typing my changes and additions to a project that I thought I could never finish.

Finally, to my friends whose help and encouragement helped me to put pen to paper: Peter Coburn, Julius Harding, Tracy Harding, Mark and Diane Holmes, Grace Martin, Jan Parkin, Julian Salt, Debbie Simpson and Patricia Taylor.

Table of Contents

Fish and Chips	9
Recovery	15
Meditation	18
Spirituality	26
Progress	29
Adjusting	40
Adjusting More	43
Different Vibrations	46
Heaven	57
Doubts	64
Understanding More	73
Controversy or Not	77
Birth	81
Rebirth	83
Destiny	85
Communication	89
What Are We?	91

Religion	94
Consciousness	97
Grief	102
Life	108
Reflections	113
Finally	118
Epilogue	122

Fish and Chips

November and December are such busy months in the run-up to Christmas. Well, they are for me, as I love decorating the house and sending out invitations for friends and family for 'get-togethers' before the big day itself.

On this occasion, the last Saturday in November, I had spent all morning in and out of the loft with what seemed like an endless number of boxes full of Christmas decorations! (I'm sure I didn't buy that much last year!) However, there they were, piled high in the spare room waiting to be displayed in all their glittering glory around the house. I made myself a cup of tea and sat down for five minutes to rest. Well, that didn't last long, my enthusiasm got the better of me and I just had to make a start by decorating the tree in the hall. You know how long these things take and several hours had passed by and the tree looked great covered in decorations, sparkling with hundreds of twinkling lights while the hall looked as if there had been an earthquake with empty boxes and packaging everywhere.

Oh well, no gain without pain, I'd better clean this mess up and get supper ready, it's later than I thought. Oh dear, it's already getting dark and I'm not in the mood for cooking; I'll phone a few friends and see if they want to come round for fish and chips and watch a film. "Great idea, love to," was the reply.

"Ok, you go and choose the film and I'll get the fish and chips."

We all arrived back at the same time, I with the delicious aroma from the chip shop and they with what I hoped was going to be a good film, what more could anyone want?

I often take an antacid tablet before eating fish and chips to prevent indigestion, and that has served me well in the past. Not so this evening; halfway through my meal, I began to feel discomfort which rapidly turned into pain, so much so, that despite my best efforts to dispel it, I had to stop eating.

"Are you OK? You don't look very well."

"Yes, fine thanks, it's just a bit of indigestion, it will go soon."

"It must be more than that, you've never left any chips before. Do you think you should phone a doctor?"

"Don't be silly, I don't want to waste a medic's time with indigestion. I'll be alright." But I had to admit I was beginning to feel quite unwell.

"Shall we call an ambulance?"

"Absolutely not, it's only indigestion."

Famous last words! Unbeknown to me one, of my dear friends, had already called an ambulance and they were at my house in less than four minutes. I was sitting by the stairs in absolute agony as the two paramedics walked in.

"Can you describe the pain to me?" One of them said in a calm voice as they wired me up to the ECG machine.

"You're having a heart attack and I need you to tell me how bad the pain is."

"Ok, it's as if my worst enemy is pushing a blunt iron bar through my chest slowly. I really don't feel well at all, I think I am going to faint, the pain is excruciating."

With that, my heart stopped thumping and went into spasm, the tightness around my chest increased and I could feel myself slowly falling forward as I lost consciousness and landed on the floor, dead.

So much happened so quickly in the next six minutes; I will recount it firstly from my friends' point of view and secondly from mine.

My friends watched helplessly as the paramedics injected me with medication and used the defibrillator three times and then gave me CPR which unfortunately broke eight of my ribs. Luckily for me, I didn't feel a thing as I was already dead. Their perseverance and skill paid off and after six minutes I began to breathe again and my heart started erratically beating as they rushed me off to the hospital for emergency surgery. Apparently, the ten-minute journey to the hospital was eventful as the lack of oxygen to my brain and erratic heartbeat were causing me to fit badly and my body was convulsing and spasming throughout the whole journey.

On arrival at the hospital, I was rushed into the operating theatre only to have another massive heart attack while they were trying to prepare me for cardiac stents. Again, my heart stopped beating, but this time, it took much longer to revive me before they could proceed with the operation. Eventually, after five hours, I was deemed stable enough to be taken to intensive care where I remained in an induced coma for five days. My friends heard the surgeon say to a senior nurse "He's in a very bad way, his heart is so damaged he has less than 1% chance of being alive in the morning."

To return to the beginning, from my perspective sitting by the stairs, I saw the paramedics come in but then had to close my eyes due to the intense pain in my chest. Strangely, despite everything going on, I became aware of a faint glow on my forehead. It was nothing much at first, just a soft light that I seemed drawn to. It had a calming effect on me despite the fact I could hardly breathe as my chest began to feel tighter and tighter and the pain became more intense.

"Are you still in pain?" The paramedic said.

"Yes," I replied, but intuitively I knew if I could just keep staring at the glow in my forehead, not only would it become brighter, but that brightness would help me to cope with the pain. My brain was starting to go into overdrive as fragments of thoughts coursed randomly through my mind:

"I can't breathe, the pain is choking me, I can't move, God help me, I'm dying. I can't be, I've got more to do. I am not dying, there's supposed to be a tunnel with a light, I can see a light but there is no tunnel, the light is just in front of me, where is the tunnel?"

It didn't occur to me I was already at the end of the tunnel and about to die—but then how many of us are that logical moments before death? Although all these thoughts were spinning in my head, I felt myself becoming quite calm. It seemed odd to be in such mental turmoil and yet feel calm, but I could not deny it, a peace seemed to be enveloping me. Suddenly my heart went into an agonising spasm contracting into a vice-like grip and stopped beating—this is when everything started to happen.

Intuitively, I wanted to do nothing except focus on the light in front of me, and for a moment, I thought I was losing consciousness but didn't. The light became brighter as my head started to slowly fall forward, but strangely at the same time, I still seemed to be sitting upright.

A random thought flashed through my mind, "I seem to be unpeeling myself like a banana," as I watched my body fall to the floor while 'I' was still sitting in the chair.

'I' looked at my body as if it were a pile of old clothes lying there. Another thought flashed through my mind; "I feel much better now I haven't got that old body anymore and the pain has gone too," and I calmly watched the paramedics give me CPR and use the defibrillator in an effort to restart my heart.

"I wish they wouldn't bother, I feel OK," but things were changing again!

My mind was finding it difficult to focus so I started to stare at my hands, "Oh, I'm still solid. If I am dead, aren't I supposed to look like a ghost?" (Strange what goes through your mind when you are recently deceased!) I looked at my body on the floor, "Yes it's still there, but it's starting to look less solid and for that matter so is everything around me. My friends, the paramedics, the hall and even my Christmas tree have all become semi-transparent—ghost-like even—but not me, I am as solid as I always was." But the light I was focussing on in my forehead was all around me now and growing inside me.

"How beautiful this all feels. Who needs skin and bones when you can feel like this?"

I wanted to tell my friends and the paramedics, "Don't bother with that old body on the floor, I am still here on the chair," but I couldn't communicate with them no matter how hard I tried, it wasn't their fault, I suppose they couldn't see me!

So, here I was, still 'solid' me looking at my semi-transparent friends and the Christmas tree and my semi-transparent old body in my semi-transparent house, yet I was filled with a glowing light and not worried about a thing!

Well, that only lasted six minutes when suddenly I felt a strange pulling sensation in my chest, and everything became hazy. The next thing I remember is I am back in my body on the floor, in absolute agony, staring at the ceiling with a paramedic looking at me saying, "Good, we've got him back, let's get him on a stretcher and off to the hospital."

Not that I want to sound ungrateful, but I wished they hadn't tried so hard!

Oh well, such is life.

Recovery

"I must say, you have made a remarkable recovery since your procedures," said my consultant three months later.

"Thanks to you, I feel fine—really well."

"Have you experienced any unusual side effects since being discharged from the hospital?"

"No, none, just the fatigue and bits of memory loss, which are to be expected due to the oxygen starvation in my brain as they tried to revive me. Other than that, I am back to normal." Best to leave it there, I thought, until I could explain what else was happening to me.

I don't know if this is a good or a bad thing, but I am one of those people who like to be able to prove things for myself, rather than being totally reliant on others for the answers. I am sure this has made me difficult to live with, but that's the way I am, so I have to get on with it!

Well, since coming home after my cardiac episode, one day, I accidentally found I was able to repeat 'unpeeling' myself. It first became evident when I was quietly resting, my mind was recalling the evening in the hallway with the paramedics when the same sensations started happening again. It was such a shock, but thankfully, I wasn't having another heart attack! Sitting in the chair the feeling of disorientation and sense of energy flowing through my body began to make me feel quite odd, so I stood up. I don't know why I did that or why I happened to turn around and look at the chair, but I did, and there was my body still on it! My instinct was to look closely at it—me?—to see if I was still breathing! I don't know why that mattered at the time—but it did, and yes, my body was still breathing.

"Well, that's a relief, at least I know I'm not dead if I am still breathing."

I continued to stare at myself and saw my body slowly become transparent along with the chair and the rest of the room.

"Wow, this is just like dying again, but without the pain. I must be dreaming this; it can't be real."

I looked at my hands and feet, they were changing too, except they and the rest of me started off ghost-like but were now becoming more solid. What I was beginning to learn was that each dimension becomes 'solid and real' as we experience and adjust to it. In other words, the world is 'real' while we live in it and then, when we die, the next level of existence becomes 'real'. So, nothing is really solid—only to our senses at that moment. So, we don't become ghosts when we die—we remain as solid to our senses as we did on earth, but if we look back at the earth, and our loved ones, they, will look ghost-like to us, because we are vibrating on a different level to them.

"This is interesting, I hope I will be able to get back into myself again," and with that, I felt the strange pull once more and **bang**, I was back sitting in the chair, feeling dizzy and disorientated. It took me a little while to regain my equilibrium but once I had settled, I wondered if I could repeat it, but no I couldn't. "Is this going to be a spontaneous thing, randomly happening to me or will I be able to control it? The first time it happened I was dying and I really don't want to do that again, no matter how amazing it was, so I need to find a way of controlling my mind and energy. Perhaps meditation will work, I think that is what transcendental meditation is all about and I used to practice a form of meditation years previously but with little success as it didn't seem to suit me, or I didn't suit it. So, time to do some research on meditation and see if that works."

The internet can be a wonderful thing.

Meditation

Well, there certainly is some wacky stuff out there as well as the more traditional forms of meditation. How does the beginner sort the good from the bad other than through trial and error? It could take years of switching one method for another, following guidelines and rules, each seeming to contradict the previous in an endless pursuit of the 'magic key' or formula to finding lasting bliss. It all seemed a bit confusing and I wasn't too convinced.

So, time to start again. What am I wanting to achieve here? I am trying to find a way of leaving my body at will so I can experience the incredible feelings of peace and tranquillity without having to die in the process! This may be a hopeless task, but I have to try.

Now, let's look at this logically. In normal everyday life, we are most definitely stuck inside our physical bodies. I know I have left mine a couple of times each under different circumstances, so it must be possible to do it again.

Science has proven that everything is vibrating at different speeds, nothing is truly motionless, so that is what must have happened to me when I had the heart attacks. As my body stopped functioning, I—the personality—started to vibrate at a different speed to my flesh and bones and left my body behind. How this happened, I have no idea, or why it happened again by just thinking about the event is even more of a mystery. But it did happen and I am going to find out how—I hope!

Ok, I am going to try to 'transcend' my body by somehow making it vibrate at a different speed, so first I'll try some visualisation. Sitting comfortably, the process began, walking along a path over a bridge watching a stream flow towards the sea of calm. Well, it was, except my mind was too caught up with the narrative and began working overtime creating different scenarios and locations, some of which were not peaceful at all! After weeks of effort and visualisations on a theme, I was nowhere near my goal. Time to try something different.

Perhaps an empty mind will enable me to leave my body. Well, that was even more stressful. The more you try not to think, the more you keep checking to see if you are thinking and then you end up trying to observe yourself to see if there are any thoughts. So what are you doing? You've got it, you're thinking again. Even when, and if, one can get to the point of 'being in the present' and observing it, the facts of observation and experience are continuous processes and our mind is recognising these events and therefore 'working', and if we are able to completely still our mind then obviously we would be unable to recall anything that might have happened during these meditations.

Well, what's the point of that?

So, neither of these methods worked for me and there were many more that I tried but none gave me the results I was looking for.

Time to start again. Recalling what happened the first time, I remembered the incredible peace I felt as it radiated through me. Its origins came from deep within my chest.

"I think I will concentrate on that instead."

It made sense to me why the ancient ones talked about the breath so much. I think it is not a coincidence that the lungs are situated on either side of the heart. This is where I felt the peace coming from. Science says that the heart, as an organ, is incapable of feeling emotion. For that matter, there are no organs in the body that create emotions, yet we all feel them. That being so, I defy anyone to prove the heart area is not the place where we register our emotions. After all, which of us, in the course of our lives, has not experienced the emotional trauma of a broken love affair or the loss of someone close to us? Where do we register that emotion? In the heart area. Let me put it another way, we do not experience heartache in our big toe! Perhaps that is why they call it 'heartache'.

To sum up, meditation as far as I can see, will be the best way forward and it can be boiled down to two main types:

- Heart-based
- Intellect-based

Or sometimes a mixture of both.

I didn't seem to relate to intellect-based mediations at all; they filled my mind with even more thoughts than I already had—probably my fault entirely. So that left me with heart-based meditation. Time to give it a go.

Off I went to the quietest room in the house and sat comfortably in my favourite chair and let myself focus on my breathing. Nothing forced or excessive (I have asthma); just natural gentle breathing which helped me become aware of my heart area. This is where the calm originated. So what do I feel? Well, all sorts of emotions made themselves felt. This was a shock! Everything from anxiety, jealousy, sadness, fear etc., you name it, I felt it! This is not going to be as easy as I thought, but what choice is there other than to carry on, if I wish to succeed?

Ok, try again. Another load of unwanted rubbish made its emotional presence felt, I didn't realise I was such a mess! Just got to keep going and not give up. After a lot of failed experimentation, the most efficient way I found of getting past all those feelings was to take another gentle breath and let my awareness follow it even deeper into the core of my heart. This had the effect of getting me through the unwanted emotional state which then felt like a layer of negativity within me. How unusual!

When these emotions are first encountered, they seem like an insurmountable blob, stuck like granite, never to move. But after passing through them (that's how it feels), I observed they were merely wavelengths of energy related to specific incidences I had created or had happened to me. Needless to say, I didn't come across just one block of emotion—not at all—there were many, but with dedication and a single-minded sense of purpose I drew closer to the feeling I was searching for.

Before you become disheartened by the thought of facing all these buried emotions, it may help you to understand that everyone has them to a greater or lesser extent. Everyone has collected emotional baggage on their journey through life and this can be a way of dissipating it. Every memory has a corresponding emotional charge to it and just as we store memories, so we store their emotional counterparts. I have to be honest and say some of my emotions were far easier to penetrate than others. Some of the most painful took days or weeks to go beyond, but having done so they never returned and believe me, I really did look around inside myself to see if they were lurking somewhere ready to annoy me again. But no, they had gone forever even when I deliberately recalled the incident that caused them.

As the saying goes, *good riddance to bad rubbish*!

Then one day, as if all this wasn't enough, I began wondering what prompted mankind to begin these inward searches and how they formulated their findings all those thousands of years ago. Were they looking for peace, wisdom or the meaning of existence, and what made them look inward instead of outward? We will never know who they were or how they came about making their discoveries, but I felt most strongly their original ideas had a simplicity that is seldom expounded today. Some may think we have progressed spiritually since those early millennia and therefore need a more 'sophisticated and advanced' approach, but I have to disagree.

For me, the simple act of dying got me there. I didn't do anything, think anything or chant anything. I just stopped breathing! And the serenity poured through me. So, what I am trying to replicate as closely as possible, is the feeling of complete freedom before the peace made its presence felt. This I eventually found, and as I immersed my consciousness into it, with constant practice, I could gradually feel myself detaching from my physical form.

People need an uncomplicated and effective means to find an inner state of peace. In our busy everyday lives, our senses are directed outwards towards our surroundings and schedules. We are all pursuing something, whether it is caring for family, business, fame or fortune, the list can be endless. Many people devote their entire lives in pursuit of these goals only to find that even if they achieve their desires, there is something missing.

Ever the cautious individual I wanted to make sure I wasn't deluding myself in some way, so I felt the best way was to try my theories out on a couple of volunteers, and who better to try and persuade to have a go, than my friends who witnessed my temporary demise on our fish and chip evening.

To say they were less than enthusiastic was an understatement and it took quite a lot of reassurance that nothing could go wrong. After all, I had come back from the dead twice so what was there to fear? Eventually, persistence won the day and they agreed for 'research purposes only'.

Surprisingly, they found the process easy to follow and could see that, with practice, it would be possible to achieve a deep and peaceful state. But, for a first go, they did feel some benefit. Obviously, no one left their bodies that night. But as they admitted after, they didn't want that to happen anyway, "But I did feel something besides the peace, a sort of stillness, but I can't really describe it."

"Don't worry, I have come to the same conclusion and find great difficulty describing it too. I just know it exists but I cannot analyse it."

It can only be felt.

Even then it is easier to say what it is not, which is empty or frightening in any way, and with repeated practice, I understood this:

In our daily lives, our energy is projected outwards through our senses—sight, sound, taste, touch, smell—to the world around us and our lives within it. This gives a feeling of being 'anchored in and at one' with our physical frame. When we meditate, as the ancient ones did, we withdraw our attention from the five senses and direct it inwards to the heart, thereby increasing our awareness of the peace and calm contained deep within all humanity.

To summarise, this is how it is done:

1. Withdraw our attention from the five senses
2. Concentrate inwardly on the peace found within
3. Try to retain that feeling after mediation is over

Sounds simple enough as a process, which it is, but we have to practice it often to succeed and then, what do we do with it?

For me, this process has helped me to access the profound peace I experienced when I died temporarily all those months ago. For everyone else, meditation has given them an anchor of calm and tranquillity enabling them to deal with life and all its ups and downs. Some have asked me, "Is this it, is this all there is?" It is not, it is just the beginning of an incredible journey, a journey that lasts our whole life and beyond. To know you carry within you an aura of peace and tranquillity that you can access at any time will give you a feeling of serenity that is beyond price. No one else can enter that place, nor take it from you; it is for you to be with the Creator of your soul for all eternity.

So this is why meditation was formulated. To give people a tool for spiritual introspection born from a need to understand life itself, leading to the formulation of the eternal questions:

Who am I?
What am I?
How do I exist?
Why do I exist?
How do I understand?
Is there more?

Spirituality

Months passed by and I was becoming a little more proficient at leaving my body. It didn't happen every time, especially in the beginning, but 'practice makes perfect' and along with my frustrations, my inquisitive nature was also blossoming. I decided to take a look at accepted ideas on all sorts of topics to see if they still held validity, while outside myself. I don't know why these thoughts came to mind, or where they came from, but they did and little did I know where all this would lead!

So my usual way of working was this, I would first go into meditation until I was able to leave my body and then I would mentally ask a question—I say mentally ask because I didn't speak; there was no one to talk to and for that matter, I had no idea who I was asking or if 'they' could hear my thoughts. I just did it and hoped I would get a reply that I would understand. Funny how we just presume that the reply will be in the language we will understand. (Well, there isn't much point if it isn't!)

Anyway, I digress, at first, there were no answers and then one day it happened, I got a reply. At first, I thought I was making it up, but after I recovered from the shock (which incidentally, drew me straight back into my body), my logic kicked in and I realised that if I already knew the answer I wouldn't have asked the question! Once, I actually began hearing the answer when I had just started asking the question;

"I'm sorry, but I could finish asking the question before you give me the answer?"

"Why?" was the succinct reply.

Another day I asked, "What is spirituality?"

"It is the analysis of the self and one's relationship with the infinite unknown."

At first, I wondered why I had heard 'infinite unknown' but then after much thought, I realised that until I begin to understand it, the infinite is and will be unknown to me.

All of these thoughts and sometimes pictures appearing in my head are fine, but everything **must** make sense. I am too logical to believe any old rubbish (perhaps being brought up on a farm helps to keep your feet on the ground—it certainly keeps them muddy!) and I wasn't about to lose my analytical nature under the onslaught of the sheer volume of information I was receiving. So, I vowed to dissect every answer with my powers of reason, logic and common sense.

Some weeks later, I was looking at my body on the chair and I remembered all the time and energy I had spent feeding and exercising it and realised I had spent hardly any time nurturing my spirit. Of course, we all have a duty of care to our bodies, but if all our spare time is spent on the maintenance of the shell, how much time is left for what lies within?

With that question in mind, I asked, "I can see the skin and bones I inhabit on earth, but I am also something else. What is it please?" As you can see, I like nice 'simple' questions.

The reply was an immediate thought in my brain, "You are a combination of intellect and feeling."

With that, a picture also appeared of a transparent body with a head and heart glowing more brightly than the rest. Instantly, I understood these areas were responsible for our life on earth; what we think and how we feel and that each could, and did, affect the other.

This led to my next thought, "I am sure there are people on earth who are far more intellectual than emotional and vice-versa, so what is the optimum state of being?"

"A balance between the two is to be desired. Remember this: All the knowledge in the universe will not fill the heart with love, and all the love in the world needs the intellect to understand it. Earthly desires and base instincts prevent us from experiencing lasting bliss because while we are all created from the Creator's essence (there is nothing else) we need to grow in wisdom and spiritual strength to cope with the ultimate experience."

"The epicentre of our being is a mini store of divine energy. We believe we are individuals, because of our physical bodies and limited understanding of our true nature. But in truth, we are like raindrops that form part of the divine ocean of existence. Our singular identity gives us no lasting comfort, subconsciously we are all searching for some sort of unity and fulfilment. That is the essence of spirituality, the search for, and understanding of, the unquantifiable energy that infuses our very being with life."

Obviously, being able to exit my body at will has not brought enlightenment with it!

**Looks like I'm going to have
to work very hard for that.**

Progress

As I said earlier, understanding and clarity were slowly increasing with my daily meditation, but it was not a smooth ride! The flat times (times when nothing seemed to happen, or any progress be made) were not helped by my ensuing frustrations and frequent despair. Any negativity of any kind did not help me towards my objectives at all and I painfully learnt to be less temperamental.

A calm and positive approach and determination never to give up seemed to be the correct approach to this whole process and after all, my logical mind kept telling me giving up would never get me there. Not that I know where there was or what it would feel like or look like if I ever found it! At those barren times, I often felt like giving up or that I had gone as far as I could go on my spiritual quest for knowledge and should be grateful for all I had found—which I was. But it was never enough. The search for truth and the need to understand as much as I could kept driving me forward even though sometimes I wanted to stop, I couldn't. Who needs to argue with another person when you can have endless arguments at any time of day or night with yourself? And they went on for hours!

Then, when I had completely exhausted myself arguing (I was pretty good at it), the experiences would start again, often with a statement that would really make me stop and think. Such as, *Truth is a vibration waiting to be understood. Until that time we can be at odds with the universe, grasping at ideas that have no basis in fact. Understanding truth helps the individual harmonise with the universe, losing the illusion of isolation and self.*

Well, that made me stop and think and fired my determination to start again. This certainly is a bumpy ride and where do I begin? Obviously, I have to try and understand what truth is, in this context, and can probably best do this when I am outside my body because in that state I am free of the mental limitation of my earthly brain and also more sensitive to my feelings. Intuitively, I know this will be important.

So, I have to start with some undisputed facts—truths, to see what is meant by 'harmonising with the universe'.

Ok, here we go...

"It is abundantly evident I exist." With that simple statement came a clarity and a freedom in my thinking I had never before experienced, but at the same time an awareness of a glow and energy within my heart.

I'll try another one, this one should be good!

"The universe exists."

Oh! Not the sensation I was expecting. There was a glow and clarity but nothing like the intensity of the first time. OK, I'll try and be a little more specific.

"The physical and spiritual universes exist." Well, that did it. The clarity and indescribable feeling of space in my head was instantaneous, for a moment it felt like the top of my head had been blown off. As for my heart, that just seemed to flow outwards in all directions to everything around me. The experience didn't last long, maybe several seconds and then I felt it 'contract' back into me and I resumed my normal state of being. Well, almost. I couldn't think at all to begin with, but little by little my thought processes returned and I tried to process what had happened.

So far I understand this; When the glow in my heart expanded and touched the spacious clarity in my head, the two became one and flowed out of 'me' into my surroundings. I can only assume I had just experienced myself 'harmonising with the universe' and as yet, this seems the only explanation I can find.

Secondly, the mental clarity I experienced when it felt as if my head was 'blown off' wasn't any empty void but a spacious understanding. Could this have been an example of 'truth is a vibration waiting to be understood'? Again, I can find no other explanation, for in those few moments, I knew what truth was and I understood it. It was not about specifics and yet they were contained in it. It was solid and yet not, it was full of everything yet appeared empty, but most importantly it was about 'being'. Truth is about 'knowing' without the clutter of false ideas and information.

Oh dear, I hope you don't think I was under the influence of a load of hallucinogenic drugs or something because I wasn't. It's just so difficult to describe all this in everyday language when it was anything but an everyday experience. However, I must continue checking these ideas as they enter my mind. So far I think I will recognise the truth when I encounter it now that I have had the last experiences. So, what about the opposite? Will I be able to recognise false information when I come across it? Better test it and see how things go. I'll make up some statements that can't possibly be true to see if it puts me 'at odds with the universe'.

"I've got three heads."

No response, nothing.

"The moon is made of cream cheese."

Again, no response, no glow or expansion of consciousness. I know these last statements have no basis in fact so I wouldn't have expected to feel 'harmony with the universe', and that being so it does leave me with a sense of isolation, nothing dramatic, just an awareness of something being wrong. Well, I only have these simple tools to test all my experiences, I hope they will be enough for the task as I can't think of anything else to do.

So, to summarise: The truth will give me a glow and feeling of at-one-ment and incorrect images and information will register as emptiness or nothingness.

Time to try things out.

I remember a few weeks previously, I learnt intelligence and emotion are different vibrational energies and we are all a combination of both. I knew they radiated from the head and heart but how did they get there and where did the source of this energy come from?

I patiently remained in meditation waiting for some kind of answer. A great deal of time passed before an image slowly appeared in my mind of soft glowing energy everywhere. Within this glow, people appeared lying horizontally and motionless and at first, I thought they had died, but on closer examination, I could see them breathing, they were just asleep. They too were glowing and around each of them was a soft pulsing radiance. I watched fascinated as the energy all around was absorbed into their bodies. So this is why we feel refreshed after a good night's sleep. Not only are we allowing our muscles to relax by lying down, but our senses are also closed down through sleep and then everything is energised by the glow that has flowed into us.

It occurred to me there are many similarities between sleep and meditation. In both, we withdraw our energy from our senses, the only difference being that in sleep, it is an unconscious action whereas in meditation, it is a conscious one. Again, in both, we absorb this glowing energy which surrounds us and again in sleep it is a subconscious action and in meditation it is conscious.

In our waking hours, we use this energy to fill our lives with work and play and as it is used up we feel fatigue and hunger and interestingly, even the process of digestion uses energy, some of which food can provide, so we still need sleep. When we are unwell, our natural reaction to illness is to sleep and, as we age, our body becomes less efficient at storing energy, so we doze more. I include myself in this last category—like an old boiler—less energy efficient than the newer models!

So, to return to my original question; "Where does this energy come from?" I had seen it energising us while we were asleep so now I needed to know where the light itself comes from.

Looking harder at those sleeping people, everyone was vibrating as masses of energy, and upon even closer inspection, I saw it was composed of many wavelengths, all vibrating at different speeds, yet all in harmony with each other. So here was proof, no matter what our age, race, size or gender, we are all composed of the same energy. We breathe the same air, and our bodily functions are the same. We are the same species and we derive our energy from the same source. However, that still hadn't answered my question, I needed to find the source of the glow.

As you can imagine this was not going to be an easy task, especially as no information of any kind was forthcoming. So it looks like I'm going to have to find out for myself. Now, this may seem like a stupid thought but I wanted to see how far this glow stretched and if it came to an end, discover what was beyond it. If no one is giving me any answers, the only thing left for me to do is stare into the glow and see what comes of it.

Well, that was easier said than done. Every time I stared at the light, I began to feel disorientated, almost like sea sickness and this caused me to jolt back into myself every time. Looks like I've got to practise more, lots more! It did pay off eventually, the phrase 'practice makes perfect' is true after all and after a while, I found myself staring for longer and longer periods into the light. Then a strange thing started happening. As I concentrated on the light, the walls of my house lost their density and became translucent and I seemed to float through them; I wasn't walking, I was just drawn through as if being pulled along on a trolley.

"How odd, I've just passed through the walls of my house with no effort at all. I was upstairs so now I'm floating fifteen feet in the air (it couldn't have happened downstairs could it?) Oh well, I don't seem to be worried about falling, I must be going mad or dreaming or both."

Then my attention was drawn to my neighbours below me in their garden. I thought I was calling them, but they couldn't hear me, and thinking about it they couldn't see me either. Probably a good thing as they might have died of shock seeing me hover above them!

Keep staring at the light, I thought, *and don't get distracted.* Well again, that's easier said than done. However, what became clearer was that everything was glowing within this light. The more I stared, the further I travelled, out of my town, over the countryside and then the sea. How glorious it looked softly shimmering and glowing while supporting all the life forms within it. "Dare I look at the sky or will it be too much for me, but then I do have to find the source, so there is no choice—just do it!"

Nervously, I gazed upward to see it wasn't lit by the sun's light but by the same glow as everywhere else. It drew me upwards; fear had now been replaced by exhilaration and excitement as I felt myself being pulled towards the stars. The light was the same even here beyond our galaxy as I travelled ever onward into the furthest reaches of the universe. Then suddenly, the galaxies were no more, just clouds of gases replacing the countless stars.

"Can this be the end of the universe?" There, amongst the vast, faint formless wisps of nothingness floating in the ever-present golden light, I turned around—there was the universe in all its splendour, trillions of galaxies with billions of stars all suspended in magnificent and timeless grandeur. I paused in awe at the beauty of it all. "How glorious this all is, but my journey still needs to be completed. I haven't yet found the source of the golden glow and must keep my focus on that." I realised I was no longer travelling as before but just staring intently at the light.

"Is this all there was before the universe existed and if so, how did it come about?" Intuitively, my gaze was drawn deeper and deeper into the glow which was composed of thousands of vibrations with everything moving within it.

"I have to concentrate further," and in doing so, the vibrations became bigger, as if being viewed under a microscope. Then my attention was drawn to the apparent space between each undulation of energy—there was nothing to be seen—but it felt so peaceful, it was not empty.

"Can this be true, is this my imagination? Can this light, which supports all the universe, come from this apparent vacuous void?" I know I couldn't see anything, but I also knew I could feel a buoyant stillness in all those spaces.

The stillness has to have existed before the light and before creation.

The light came from the stillness.

My mind was almost exploding with myriad thoughts and realisations, *I must keep calm and above all I must be logical. I have to stare at the stillness and feel it to even begin to understand.* Then slowly, from deep within the feeling these truths entered my consciousness.

The stillness existed before time—for there was nothing to measure time by. The stillness was all there was—for nothing else existed. The stillness is unchanging—to change it has to move. The stillness supports everything—for everything came into being within it.

"Am I fooling myself staring at 'all there is', what can be trusted?"

For that matter, what can any of us trust, only our senses and logic, how else do we assess anything?

I have travelled from my body, through the countryside and over the sea, passed planets and galaxies to the end of the universe and stared at the light. Even that revealed its wavelengths were infused with, and supported by the eternal stillness.

"Is there more?"

Those words drew me ever closer to the stillness as I felt myself dissolving slowly but surely into the light. It felt as if I was letting go of who I was, what I thought, and was melting into all there was. My body became the merest mist-like form until I was unaware of its presence altogether.

How can I describe the indescribable, how can my tiny little brain with my limited vocabulary possibly convey the exhilaration and peace I was feeling? There are no words to convey the immensity of the experience, I just had to feel it. *I must try to keep calm for I know that too much emotion will pull me back into my physical body.*

What is this experience? I need to understand. Can science help me? I'm not sure. How can you quantify the unquantifiable when there are no parameters anywhere? What about the religious viewpoint, can I possibly be approaching the Creator of all life and light itself, the all-seeing and unknowable, the eternal life force that men call God? I am not worthy, I am no saint. There are many more compassionate and caring people than I am. If I am truly here, I feel I don't deserve to be. I am just an ordinary person who has led an ordinary life, not rich or famous, cruel or selfish and I try to help others when I can. Yet here I am, what other explanation can there be? I will not delude myself, so I will try to let go of all that I am and surrender myself to the unknown.

As I became ever calmer, I could feel myself losing my identity until I was just a point of awareness in the vast stillness of eternity. I could experience all things simultaneously, but the experiences seemed to contradict themselves.

"There appears to be a void and yet it is full, there is no movement yet there is a buoyancy everywhere. There is no light, yet there is a brightness greater than any I have ever seen." The nothingness and the everything combined into oneness and vaporised into stillness and serenity, I was lost in the immediacy and joyous freedom of it all.

I cannot tell you how long this lasted, eternity wouldn't be long enough, but I knew I couldn't think and didn't want to, I could only experience.

Eventually, thoughts and emotions invaded the stillness, disturbing the tranquillity and peace. Then a faint glow appeared, forming miniscule points of light which joined together to reform my astral body. My consciousness too began to 'reform' itself as my thoughts started to analyse the experience.

I don't want this to end yet—I don't want to be 'me' again, let me stay a while and experience the vast oceanic depths of creation.

No, it was not to be, it was as if my plea to remain facilitated the exact opposite happening because I felt a pull within the centre of my being while travelling backwards past all I had seen; galaxies, planets, stars, oceans and towns, back into my body with a thud.

Oh dear, how old it feels!

Adjusting

I couldn't sleep for seventy-two hours and hardly felt any need for food at all as I seemed to be living on the energy stored within me. Well, that didn't last, as gradually the pangs of hunger made their presence felt, *Damn*! I thought *I never need cook again. Oh well, just get on with life. I have obligations to fulfil so obviously being an aesthetic in lonely contemplation on the meaning of life is not my destiny*! My musings were interrupted by the phone as usual!

"Are you OK? We haven't seen or heard from you in a few days."

"Yes, I am fine."

"Well, you don't sound it, we are in the area so let us pop in, just to make sure."

"Ok, if you want to, it would be nice to see you all, but I really am OK."

Five minutes later, they were in my kitchen with some flowers.

"Well, you look OK, but something is different."

Dare I tell them, or will they think I've lost it completely? Oh, what the hell, I'll go for it.

"Let's go into the breakfast room and sit down, I've got something to tell you. Oh, and bring your tea, you're going to need it!"

An hour and a half later, my friends were sitting in complete silence like budgies on a perch, staring at me with their mouths wide open.

"It's OK, I won't struggle, just give me a few minutes to pack some things and you can have me committed to the asylum straight away."

"What do you mean, have you committed?"

"Well, none of you said a word the whole time I was speaking and you're looking at me as if I have grown two heads."

"Sorry for staring but we didn't want to interrupt you, it sounded so unbelievable, yet I think I speak for all of us when I say I know you're not lying because, as strange as it seems, it all feels so true."

"Please don't be kind because I have been ill," although I did need reassurance as I was feeling quite insecure.

"No, we are not being kind, we are being honest. Has anything else happened that you can tell us about?"

"Do you really want to know, how long have you got?"

"Of course, we want to know and why didn't you tell us about your experiments with leaving your body before now? Why was everything such a secret?"

"Well, I wasn't sure about anything in the beginning and wondered if it was my brain playing up due to oxygen starvation during the heart attacks."

"Of course, we understand that and your need to be sure, but you've seen and done things most people can only wonder about. Anyway, you have a knack for explaining things that makes them easy to understand."

"Oh, thanks."

Eventually, they went home, but not before a ten-minute battle of wills—which I lost—and a promise to have them back the following week to continue the story. I did make them agree to bring some questions with them next time, after all, a conversation is a two-way thing and I wasn't going to do all the work.

Adjusting More

"Thanks for a lovely evening. Can we bring a couple of friends next time?" was the question asked as my friends left after two hours of me constantly talking.

"Ok, but I am not too sure about this. It's a serious topic for me, not just a conversation point."

"We know that. These people are really interested in what you have to say. One has just lost her husband and the other, her mother some months ago and we are sure your experiences of dying and that life goes on afterwards will be of great comfort to them."

"Ok then. I know I can help them understand the process of dying and hopefully take some of the trauma away. But please make one thing clear before they arrive; I am not an intermediary between them and their loved ones. I am not able to give messages from the other side. That is not my thing. If they want to contact their loved ones, perhaps they should visit a clairvoyant or medium, someone who is far better equipped for that job than I am. Is that clear?"

"Yes, absolutely, they just want to hear your story."

"Alright then, bring them with you next week and I will tell them my story and try to answer their questions."

Oh dear, what have I let myself in for? I hope I am able to help them.

I needn't have worried. The two strangers arrived with my friends the following week. Each told me their individual story of tragic loss and the heartache it brings, of how empty life seems afterwards and how many questions cannot be answered.

"Maybe my own story will help answer some of your questions. I can describe the physical process of dying to you and how I felt emotionally afterwards, but I cannot take the pain of your grief away. Knowledge about the process of death can diminish some of the fear of the unknown, and knowing they are out of pain and are OK, even though you can't see them, can be a great comfort. But, grief is matched only by the amount of love you have for someone. If you don't care, it doesn't hurt. From my personal experiences, I know pain stops completely the second we cease breathing. I will also go so far as to say that as we approach our last moments on earth the pain is already subsiding and more importantly, when we actually leave our body and cease breathing, we are not wispy and ethereal or ghost-like. We leave the old body behind and we recognise our self as 'still solid' and it is this continuation of 'form' that gives us a feeling of security that we still are who we always were."

"Why do some people say they have seen a ghost-like spirit arising from someone's body when they die?"

"Because when you die, your 'flesh and bone body' remains vibrating at its usual speed, which is the same rate that you are vibrating at, so you see it and yourself as solid. But death releases the person from their body and they then vibrate at a faster rate than the skin and bones they have just left behind. This increase in vibration makes them seem ghost-like to those on earth who are able to see them or to put it another way, you are still you, whether you are wearing your physical overcoat or not. Another thing you ought to know is there is no fear, only peace, which can take a little getting used to."

"Does everyone feel this peace?"

"I'm not sure. I'll try and find out and tell you next week."

Why do I say these things?

Different Vibrations

Resuming my morning meditations the next day, leaving my body was far easier than usual so I decided to ask a question, "Are there different places or vibrations to the one I have already experienced?"

There was a pause and I was certainly not prepared for the answer. I wasn't told, neither did it appear in picture form; I was taken there. I don't know how or who by, but there was definitely someone behind me because I could feel them.

I felt us plummet endlessly downwards and the deeper we went the darker and thicker the atmosphere became until it felt as if we were immersed in a thick black tar.

"This isn't tar," the person with me said, reading my thoughts. "The atmosphere we are in is composed of anger, loathing, bitterness and cruelty. A poisonous cocktail of some of humanity's worst emotions and thoughts swirling in a suffocating glutenous dark mass that permeated everything."

"Why am I here, I can barely move or think. Who or what could live in this disgusting place?"

"Not what, but who? This place is reserved for those souls of an evil disposition who have committed atrocities while on earth. Here and here alone, they prey on each other in their depravity and madness, for they drive themselves and each other into a never-ending cycle of aggression."

"How long do they remain here?"

"Until they have experienced the exact amount of pain, fear and anguish they caused their victims to suffer. As they experience these emotions, their negative karma lessens and hopefully, with it, the desire to cause others harm, but even then they cannot leave this place until their victims have forgiven them. Then and only then can they move to a less desperate place. No amount of pleading alters the precise balance of action and reaction. This thick atmosphere has been created by the negative vibrations of vast numbers of souls. It is a mistake to think it was created for them, it was created by them over millennia by their own actions. The divine law is exact and unalterable and as each individual's debt is repaid, they are able to slowly float to the top of the morass where others are waiting to escort them forward for rehabilitation. No one is left alone on the road to recovery. Contrition and a sincere and deep-felt desire to improve themselves are the qualities needed for this to take place, and unlike your physical world, no one can disguise their true intentions."

"I do understand what you are saying, but can we please leave as I can hardly breathe, and I really don't like it at all." With that, I was jerked back into my body and felt quite shaken and needed to seriously readjust myself. I wanted to meditate but was frightened, probably needlessly, that if I did it would happen all over again, and I would end up down there.

"I think I'd better do something physical. That should help me get my equilibrium back. Gardening should do it."

It was that or bake a cake and as cakes are fattening, the garden won!

The following day, I didn't know whether to resume my meditations or not, but after much thought, my inquisitive nature overcame any reservations I had.

Leaving my body was fairly easy which made me feel a little nervous, but as I am a glutton for punishment and needed to know more, I mentally asked, "There must be other dimensions besides the one we visited yesterday. Is it possible to see any of them?"

Again, there was a pause, no reply, but there was someone behind me as I recognised the feeling from yesterday. Suddenly we started falling again.

"Oh please, not that place again."

Seconds later, we stopped the downward journey. At least this time we weren't in the darkness, but it wasn't exactly light either. Instinctively, I turned round to talk to whoever it was behind me—there was no one there but I could still feel them behind me.

"Why are you hiding? Are you some dark force that doesn't want me to see them?"

"No, I am not a dark force and I am glad you have eventually asked the question as this brings up a fundamental point of spiritual understanding for you. You are beginning your own spiritual journey, one of self-discovery and of your relationship with God and creation. You will see many wonderful things, but it is the 'feelings' you have within those experiences that will help you to understand things that can never be seen on earth. So, because of that, I am not allowing you to see me visually, nor am I giving any information about myself until you have learnt to sense my presence and recognise it fully."

"You have already begun this process, but you must now learn to trust your instincts above anything else. You may at times, see or hear things that could mislead you, but you must now know that if you listen to and understand those feelings deep within yourself, you will stay firmly on the path God has created for you. This does not mean you will avoid all pain or mental anguish in your life if that is what you deserve, but any difficulties encountered along life's journey will be lessened by your understanding of the divine will."

"Oh, thank you, I certainly wasn't expecting that in this God-forsaken place."

"That is exactly the point I have just been making. Although this place seems 'God-forsaken' as you put it, in fact, God is everywhere, holding it together, just as the dark place you saw yesterday is held by God's love."

"At this moment in time, it's very difficult to comprehend that God would hold together places like that."

"Remember, yesterday I told you the souls in question created its darkness, not God. God merely allows those places to exist so those of his creation who have chosen to be cruel or evil are prevented from doing more harm to themselves and others by remaining there until their bad thoughts have ceased to dominate their consciousness and actions, and therefore they stand a better chance of not reoffending."

"Thank you again, and I do apologise for thinking you were maybe an evil soul out there to 'get me'. However, this isn't a particularly nice place either. It reminds me of a cold winter morning with grey skies and lots of mist. There are lots of buildings over there; it looks like a war zone, everything seems to be bombed out, and what is it about the atmosphere? It seems so lonely and depressing and there are a few people over there wandering about. What is the matter with everyone? They are doing nothing and ignoring each other. It's as if no one else exists, just them, no one is talking, and everyone looks so miserable."

"People like these have been mean and self-absorbed in the past, so when they die they find themselves in places like this, grey, uninspiring and desolate until they stop their obsessive introspective thoughts and decide to ask for help to change their ways. Help is always at hand, but the only way they can begin to alter themselves is to ask first. This is so hard for them to do for they are caught in the vice-like grip of their own negativity and do not wish to be beholden to anyone, for anything. It is their choice, so there they must remain in their own self-created isolation until they choose otherwise."

"Are there many places like this?"

"Enough to accommodate man's negativity."

"How do they arrive here; surely, no one in their right mind would want to be in a place like this!"

"They come here because their thoughts and actions have brought them here."

"Yes, I understand that, but could you tell me how please?"

"I will try to put this simply. We are like magnetic sources of energy and every thought, word and deed radiates outwards from our bodies in the form of wavelengths of energy, which then find their way back to us, rather like experiments you probably did at school with magnets and iron filings. These energetic memories are stored within our energy field for the duration of our earthly life, only to be released upon our death. But that is not the end of the story; it is just the end of a single chapter of our existence, an earthly chapter. The energy that is released upon our death of all our earthly thoughts and deeds is of two basic types. The first, a faster brighter vibration is an indicator of all the good a person has done in their lives."

"The other, a slower vibration, seems darker by comparison and represents the bad things done in a person's life. So obviously, the more good a person has done will have the effect of 'lifting' the soul upwards to a place that resonates with their soul vibration, and conversely, those whose actions are of a more negative kind will find themselves being drawn 'down' to a place that suits them as well. I have used very simple analogies here to help you understand for there are many factors to add to this complicated process, but this is the basic principle."

"Does this apply to everyone?"

"Yes, there is no escape. You are the sum total of all you have done while on earth. You cannot lie your way out of this and neither can you rid yourself of this negativity by trying to cast it off. Its energy remains with you even though it has been released from its subconscious prison when you died. Its magnetic properties mean it returns to surround you afterwards until you change your thought patterns and make amends in whichever way is applicable, thereby cutting off its energy source. Sounds easy enough, but it is not a five-minute job. It can take many years to effect a change. Until then, it is there for all to see, good deeds give souls a radiance and a joyous place to exist, while the weight of negative deeds means those souls inhabit darker realms and radiate an ugliness of spirit which cannot be disguised."

You reap as you sow.

"Hmm, memo to self—better keep positive if I don't want to end up here! Can I ask another question? What about Mr and Mrs Average who have led uneventful lives, other than what most people would accept as normal, you know—house, garden, jobs friends and family that sort of thing? What happens to them at the end of their life on earth?"

With that, I felt myself moving upwards again, out of the grey desolation we were in, and into a place so similar to my hometown I thought I was back on earth.

"Where are we now?" I asked as I struggled to re-orientate myself and recognise some familiar landmark or other. Everything looked familiar except it wasn't. There was a lovely bright sky but no sun to illuminate it. There were buildings like any town or city in a varying mixture of styles and sizes. There seemed to be shops and cafes, roads and green spaces with seats for people to enjoy nature and talk. There were people walking about and others sitting and talking—all seemed happy enough, with everything 'as normal' as one would expect. "If this isn't earth, what is everyone doing?"

"They are leading their lives as they always did."

"But don't they realise they have died?"

"No, not in the deepest sense. When they awake from death, places like this are so familiar to them they adjust very quickly and remember, their bodies are as solid to them as they always were on earth."

"But don't they have any memory of getting old or dying, and what about those they have left behind?"

"Because their form is strong and well, any memories of age, illness and death soon fade away, just as the memory of any bad dream fades from your memory upon awakening. Yes, there is a sense of loss of their loved ones but remember, any people, especially family and friends who have predeceased them, are always there to greet these new arrivals and help them adjust to their new surroundings. That is what you saw some of those people doing sitting on the park benches. They had arrived over here some time ago and were talking to others in an effort to understand their new life."

Well, that did it! My mind was now racing and full of questions about the practical details of being here.

"Do people here need to sleep, feel hungry or go to the bathroom? Do they have homes of some kind and what about working and holidays?"

"People at this level of understanding can resume as many of their earthly routines as they wish until they realise they don't need to do them anymore. Everyone has free will, and here people are only limited by the degree of their spiritual enquiries. But to answer your question, I will say this—on earth, your life is dictated mostly by your physical needs, so when you are tired you go to sleep. You only eat when you feel hunger and go to the bathroom when your body tells you so. Any other free time is then spent working or on pleasurable pursuits, hobbies, and family life. This is the construct of their life on earth, their own reality because they know no other."

"So why should it be so different over here, life is life and reality is reality, no matter where you are. This place seems so familiar to you because it is constructed from the memories of countless thousands of people who have found themselves here after death. There are many opportunities for the individual to learn the truth of existence if they so wish—there is no obligation or pressure from anyone to do so, just as on earth people can enquire about life and their spiritual nature—but how many bother? How many souls fill their waking hours in the pursuit of trivia and possessions, only to relinquish them when they die? I cannot tell you how many thousands of souls bitterly regret wasting their time on earth."

"You have just said there are many opportunities for people to learn, what are they?"

"Quite simply, it could be from a seemingly inconsequential conversation with someone who has been here longer than them, or the more obvious instances of lectures, classes and philosophical books. Everything is of an informal nature as this is the best way for them to absorb the truth without feeling inadequate or left behind in any way. Often though, while souls are full of enthusiasm to meditate upon arrival, the old habits can soon resurface to resume their place uppermost in a person's consciousness, and so meditational practice gradually loses its importance and becomes an infrequent past-time. That does not matter, there is no one to judge or condemn, for one day everyone makes the required effort, perhaps when all their friends and family have moved along the spiritual pathway and they are left alone. That is usually when they resume the meditation with a renewed sense of purpose."

"Thank you for all of this information, but I am still trying to come to terms with the fact that this place is so like earth. Are you sure I am not dreaming?"

"No, you are not dreaming, any more than you are dreaming when you perceive yourself as 'awake' in your daily life on earth. All people born on earth 'see' it as real and solid, their consciousness remembers no other reality, they feel the warmth of the sun and the cooling breeze and rain, they observe majestic mountains and can swim in the seas, feel hard stones and the heat in flames. Everything is real to their senses as it is for them after they have died, no matter where they find themselves. Every dimension is as real to its occupants as the next and that is where all remain until they evolve and move onwards."

"Do people in those darker places ever try to escape? I am sure I would try."

"Yes, they try constantly but the apparent darkness and weight of their energy field is so interwoven with their surroundings that escape is impossible. Remember that tar-like atmosphere we visited? It does not come with doors or windows to escape through or pathways to run down, it is almost a sealed unit in itself containing only those who created it. They cannot claim they have been wrongly accused or do not deserve to be in that place. There are no clever lawyers to argue their case on technicalities and points of law. Unlike earth, divine law cannot be misinterpreted or twisted to suit a criminal's needs, not in any way. Divine law is perfect in itself and for the benefit of all."

"So how can they rid themselves of this darkness? It must take forever."

"No, not forever, but it will take a very long time, remember they are surrounded by likeminded souls, so change for them is very difficult. They have to alter their habitual thinking to become out of harmony with their surroundings. It is the only way they have to leave its magnetic pull."

"A little more information on the reality of death; we, over here, are always made aware of someone's impending demise. Whether they are good or bad, their death is sudden or unexpected or the result of a long illness or long life, when a soul leaves its body for the final time, two or three of us are waiting nearby to assist in their passing. This happens for every soul, every time. Now, most newly deceased souls are only too willing to come with us to the next dimension and be with their loved ones who have gone before them. But there are some who simply refuse to come with us no matter how hard we try to help them. They say they are not dead and wish to remain where they are. However, as you well remember when your heart stopped beating, one second you were in your body and the next you were not. The physical change is rapid but for these souls, the mental adjustment is not, so reluctantly we have to leave them where they are until such time as they call out for help, which is given immediately, and assist them to fully join us in the next dimensions."

Heaven

Having spent several days recovering mentally and emotionally from recent experiences, it wasn't long before my inquisitive nature was at it again and not wanting to go on any more visits to dark places, I was very careful how I asked the next question:

"Is it possible to visit more beautiful realms than those I have already seen, and who lives there?"

No reply.

"Perhaps everyone is busy or something. I'll give it five minutes then try again."

Ten minutes passed, still silence, "Perhaps I have asked too much, or I am not allowed to see. I wonder if I have done something wrong. There must be something not right, I can't leave my body and feel quite dizzy and a bit nauseous."

"Have I done something wrong? If so, please tell me."

"Calm down and stop struggling. You need to be fully focused on your heart centre within, in order to be able to travel to, and remain in, the upper realms for any length of time. Anyway, you have already managed to travel beyond the boundaries of the physical universe and experienced immersing yourself in the divine presence by letting go of all your thoughts and emotions. This is just another way of drawing close to that experience again and you are making things difficult for yourself."

"Hmm, no words of encouragement today."

"Why do you need encouragement? Is not the fact you can visit these places and have all this knowledge freely given to you incentive enough? Why do you need your ego massaging as well?"

"No, of course, I don't, I am afraid my ego survives all too well without any help at all. I am sorry if my thoughts caused offence, although I did think they were private."

"You have been given the ability to travel almost wherever you wish in the universe. The price for this is that we must have access to your every thought, so you may come to no harm unintentionally. Your spirit is attached to your physical body by a fine cord of energy which stretches from your body's forehead to your spirit's forehead when you are on your travels, no matter where they may be. It is this cord, which some on earth call the astral cord, that enables your physical body to stay alive when you are absent from it. When that energetic cord is severed, your body dies and you will join us permanently over here. Before you ask, yes I know, you have died twice already, so yes, your cord was severed but it was re-energised so you can continue your earthly life."

"I see you have no trouble reading my thoughts."

"You are nothing if not predictable! However, you were not fully paying attention and your thoughts interrupted me, so I will continue. While you are still attached to your body by this cord, your consciousness does not always absorb information as fully, or indeed as rapidly as it will when you are completely free. Therefore, this sometimes makes you vulnerable when visiting lower levels. Remember, we have a spiritual responsibility for your well-being."

"Don't worry, I have no intention of going anywhere near places like that ever again!"

"We are aware of your intentions, but nothing is left to chance. So let us resume where we left off and I want you to focus your concentration fully within, and when you are sufficiently energised, I will be able to show you sights you will not believe."

It's amazing how the anticipation of something great happening can focus the mind, and I could feel a sense of excitement welling up within me, but I was also aware of the fact that 'I must keep as calm as possible or this will not work.'

"Can I ask just one thing before we begin?"

"You may."

"If I was allowed to travel to the very edge of creation and beyond, and then to merge with the infinite on my own...why am I having to prepare for the upper realms with you to assist me?"

"You were not alone! Also, I wish you to be able to remain in the upper realms for longer than you were able to merge with the infinite. You must build up your store house of energy—so concentrate!"

It didn't take long for the accumulated energy in my heart area to make me feel dizzy and a little nauseous, not the best of feelings and certainly one I wasn't expecting.

"Why do I feel sick? Am I doing something wrong?"

"The accumulated energy in the heart area is what is making you nauseous. Under normal circumstances, you would have easily left your body by now, but I am preventing that so you may stay longer in the upper realms, as I said earlier."

By now, the accumulated energy within me was pouring itself into my whole body making me feel lighter and brighter as I once again separated from my form and felt myself floating upwards into the unknown.

"Oh great, this is just how I felt when I approached the infinite."

"You need to concentrate fully. Do not let your thoughts become distracted."

"Oh, caught again!"

"We are here, please open your eyes slowly for you will find the light bright indeed."

"You're not kidding, I can't see a thing, it's far too bright."

"I did warn you. Close your eyes again for a few moments and then try once more."

This time, I was much more cautious yet the first thing I noticed, even before I opened my eyes, was the atmosphere. It is difficult to describe, but the words most suitable are buoyant and fragrant, buoyant in the sense I felt weightless but not floating and fragrant in the sense of pure mountain air, but even better. Slowly my eyes began to focus and what really hit me was the realisation that the light was actually full of this buoyancy and fragrance. It was a strange thing to understand, yet here it was, and I could feel the three things were indivisible.

In this glorious feeling, shapes and forms came into focus and everything possessed a radiance and luminescence that was overwhelming. The crystal clarity of the colours, even some that are not seen on earth, was breath-taking. The majestic serenity of the distant mountains and the sparkling waters of the lakes and rivers were like those on earth, just far more beautiful. There were buildings as well, gleaming white in classical styles and so in harmony with the surrounding countryside I hardly noticed them there at all. Nothing offended the eye, but more important than the visual splendour was the feeling of love and joy, which permeated everything.

How serene this all is, what peace and love fills the air. This truly is paradise.

There were people in the Sylvian landscape sitting in quiet contemplation or in small groups, some were walking amongst the flowers and fields of grasses. They were communicating telepathically for I saw their faces become animated, but no words came from their lips.

"In these upper realms, objects are given form by the focussing of thought, meaning the mind of the individual can harness the energy available (actually it's limitless) and condense it until it appears solid and remains so for as long as is required. In less exalted realms, this is not possible because the inhabitants do not have the knowledge or mental discipline to achieve this, so they need to achieve results in the same way as on earth for this is the only way they remember working."

"In even lower realms, buildings appear derelict or almost transparent due to lack of interest and the ability of the inhabitants. These souls do not care for their surroundings for they are too preoccupied with their own cravings, problems and negative outlook. They do not care about their surroundings and so, with time, the energy stored up in these objects and buildings begins to dissipate back into the ether—hence the almost transparent appearance of their surroundings."

"How I wish I could remain here in this upper realm."

"Just here? There are other realms even finer than this, but I doubt if you would be able to perceive their beauty and splendour due to the intensity of the light. I know you experienced the ultimate peace as you plunged into the infinite, but you were unable to remain there for any length of time, and your consciousness and soul could not grasp even the smallest fraction of the divine experience. These finer realms I speak of are the merest whisper away from the ultimate bliss. They too are solid, but solid light, which the souls that inhabit them can dissipate at will into the infinite. Their spiritual attainment is beyond the average man's understanding, for they are in a permanent state of divine ecstasy which does not render them incapable. Far from it, to be able to gaze into their eyes you realise they understand all things, everything is within their grasp, for they are at one with the Creator."

"How did they become so spiritually advanced? I feel as if I have wasted my life on pointless pursuits."

"They are older than you spiritually, much like older brothers and sisters, so they have had more time to work out their earthly desires and then pursue their spiritual enquiries. Everyone climbs the spiritual mountain in their own time, and when they are ready to do so. There is no race to the top, it is a voluntary choice by each to climb the ladder. Understanding oneself and one's relationship with the creative life force is the most difficult, and yet the most rewarding thing we will ever do. Our thoughts are the only thing we take with us when we die."

"Then, if it is the only worthwhile thing to do, why is it so difficult?"

The process itself is not difficult, but mankind makes it so by refusing to acknowledge that progress only comes with a change in thought and attitude. It is only when we begin to eradicate the habit of negative thinking and replace it with a positive approach to life and truth that we begin the upward climb. While I use the phrase 'upward climb', I am perhaps giving you a false image of the process. It is actually an 'inward journey', yet another image I know, but this time a more accurate one. We must analyse the thoughts and emotions that prevent us from experiencing divine bliss and couple that with meditative practice as a means of getting there. We need both. Think about it, thought alone will not fill your heart with love and without wisdom, you cannot find the ultimate destination. Many think of faith as the way of making the journey and I agree, without knowledge, faith is certainly a motivational force. But I ask you this, which is the stronger:

I Believe

or

I Know

(But just make sure that which you know, is true!)

Doubts

Have you ever doubted, or second-guessed yourself at all? You know the kind of thing. Did I just see that, or did I hear correctly? It could be anything at all; should I do this or say that? Well, you might have guessed by now I have been questioning myself a lot since being ill. My life has changed so much and so rapidly, physically with the heart attacks and mentally and emotionally with all the spiritual experiences, that I would often have prolonged periods of self-doubt. Even using my powers of logic and common sense (and my mad sense of humour) to analyse all I had seen and heard was not enough to deal with the sheer volume of experiences in my consciousness. So, just at the point of overload, as if by magic, everything would stop, and I would get a breathing space to catch up. I did wonder if my experiences were the result of oxygen depletion in my brain when having heart attacks, so I had my cognitive functions checked out at the hospital. After several tests, the results came back that, apart from long-term memory loss, everything was fine.

Well, that was news to me! "My brain is alright. I must remember to tell my friends."

The point of my telling you all of this is I had been going through one of those less-than-positive periods. I seemed to be stuck in my meditation, so questioned the process to see if

I was doing anything wrong. I wasn't able to leave my body at all and if on the rare occasions, I did manage to, the whole experience was distorted and short-lived and so day after day, I carried on in the hope that it would pass. Failure became a constant companion, and I could think of little else as doubt raised its ugly head. Did I imagine the whole thing? "Has it gone forever, how do I regain what has been lost?"

Still nothing—empty as if nothing happened.

One night I went to bed as usual with failure on my mind, and needless to say, I couldn't sleep. Now, you have no idea what a big deal this is for me. My whole life I have only taken one or two deep breaths and I am gone. My friends say I could sleep on a clothesline, and if I have to take three deep breaths, then I am having a really bad night. Back to the night in question, having lost count of the number of deep breaths I had taken I wondered if I was starting to hyperventilate—no I wasn't. I was beginning to become dizzy and disorientated when suddenly there was a massive pull in my chest and I shot out of my body like a cork from a bottle.

"Wow, whatever caused that, worked. Now what do I do?"

With that, I felt myself travelling upwards through the roof of my house and into the night sky.

"What a lovely cloudless sky!" Looking downward, my own town passed beneath me and my rate of travel began to increase.

"Here comes the water again. That was quick, back on land now, where am I going? Is anyone with me, and why aren't I frightened?"

No reply.

A vast range of mountains came into view, the snow-capped peaks gently shining in the moonlight.

"Is this the Rocky Mountains? No, they can't be. I think I have just passed over Europe, so this must be the Alps. The Rockies are in the other direction! Oh, I have just had a thought, I hope nobody drops me! What is the matter with me? Here I am flying through the night sky, seemingly on my own, not knowing where I am going or why, wondering if the mountains beneath me are the Alps or the Rockies and then randomly worrying about being dropped by someone, whoever 'they' may be, or if 'they' are even there in the first place! Weird how my mind works under stress!"

"Ahead are more mountains, this range is vast, it has to be the Himalayas. Why am I here, I don't know anyone and there is no one about anyway?"

That instantly stopped my travels and I ended up standing on a snowy ledge. It was already snowing but now it was becoming really heavy. Looking at my pyjamas, they were still dry, and for some reason, the snow wasn't settling on them and making them wet.

"That's strange, I forgot to put my slippers on. I never do that and now I am standing in the snow. This cannot be real; it has to be a dream because nothing makes sense. Why would I be standing on a snowy mountain ledge in bare feet and anyway, I bet I haven't left any footprints." I had, just shows how wrong you can be in life! "It's even crunching as I walk on it. Well, I hope this doesn't go on too long, there's nobody about, so what's the point of being here unless I am being punished in some way for doubting everything? Oh, don't start panicking, it won't do any good and anyway, someone will come and get me—eventually, I hope!"

"Perhaps I ought to find some shelter somewhere, I don't want to get frostbite on my feet because they are already numb. What the hell am I talking about frost bite and numb feet for? This really has to be some kind of alternate reality if it isn't a dream. Nobody stands up here in bare feet without getting hypothermia. Just stop thinking rubbish and concentrate on walking along the ledge, it's very slippery and who knows how far down it drops? Perhaps I should have a look and find out." Well, that was a mistake!

"I am obviously much higher up than I thought, there is no way I can see the bottom. I wasn't frightened before, but I certainly am now. My body is starting to shake with fear, or is it cold? Stop, stop, stop, just get a grip and think logically. I have been brought here for a purpose and whatever that purpose is, eventually I will find out. No one gets put on top of a mountain without shoes for nothing! So, whatever the plan is, it doesn't include falling down a crevasse, so it's not going to happen."

"Keep going, one foot after another. Just do it! There is a corner just ahead, let's see what is beyond that." Negotiating the bend wasn't easy because of the snow, however, I was motivated now by the sight of a glow in the distance.

"There must be other people up here, I wonder what they are up here for? Oh well, the only way to find out is to ask, so I hope someone can speak English. What on earth am I going to say to them? 'Hello, I am from England and I am lost up here in my pyjamas.' I don't think that is going to work at all, supposing they don't understand English, what then? Better just carry on and see how it goes."

Getting closer to the glow, I was able to see twelve figures sitting on the ground in a circle. The narrow path had widened by now to a comfortable ledge so there was plenty of room for me to stand about ten feet away from them. It was still snowing heavily, but like me, they were untouched by it.

"That's odd; it must be some kind of snow that doesn't touch anyone up here. It certainly feels warmer, it must be coming from their campfire." But I couldn't see one. "Where is the warmth and for that matter, the glow coming from? It's got to come from something up here." So I looked once more at the group. It was coming from them—they were glowing. "They can't be, it must be all this snow distorting my vision. Perhaps a closer look will reveal the answer. It is coming from them, each of them is radiating a soft luminescence. How is this possible? How can people glow in the dark? This can't be happening." I stood motionless, totally dumbstruck by the vision in front of me, for what seemed like an eternity.

"Why are you here, my son?" The voice came from everywhere and nowhere at the same time.

"I don't know. One minute I was trying to get to sleep and the next thing I knew I was pulled out from myself and ended up here in the snow in my pyjamas."

"You were worried about your meditation. That is why you couldn't sleep."

"Yes, you are right, but how could you possibly know that? I live in England."

"I know all your thoughts, my son."

"Oh, I am sorry for that. But how do you know my thoughts, I don't even know you."

"No need for apologies, my son. You are climbing the same spiritual mountain we all climbed before you, we have all stumbled at times."

Another question was forming in my mind but stopped because suddenly I found myself sitting cross-legged in the centre of the group.

"I am so sorry, I don't know how I got here. I was standing over there a moment ago and I didn't mean to disturb your peace."

"Be quiet, my son, just observe and absorb."

So, observe I did, all three hundred and sixty degrees without turning my head, seeing each and every one of them simultaneously. How, I don't know, but everyone was visible to me and in great detail. The silence was truly golden as no one moved or spoke, they just remained motionless, glowing in deep meditation. Then slowly, one by one they opened their eyes and stared at me.

"We will demonstrate the mechanical process of the meditation you have found my son, observe closely."

With that, they each closed their eyes and focused their attention on their foreheads which began to glow more brightly than the rest of their bodies. Then, slowly, they all became semi-transparent.

"This is unbelievable, it's just so unbelievable."

"Be still, my son, quieten your thoughts and observe fully with all your concentration."

Again, my thoughts were being answered in thought form, for no one moved or spoke, but I could hear someone's voice inside my head. It then became obvious why I had to concentrate, for each soul began to pulsate with light from their spinal columns. It had started in their foreheads and travelled down towards their hearts in unison. The ability to focus on the heart area made them begin to pulsate with a brilliant light which lit up their whole being. I couldn't help it, so I started talking to myself again.

"This can't be real; it has to be a dream."

"It is not a dream. Focus."

By now, the light within each of them was so bright it felt like looking directly at the sun.

"I can't do this for much longer, the light is blinding me."

"Yes, you can—calm yourself and observe."

The brilliant light from their heart centres began to expand beyond their bodies until it joined in one blinding circle of overwhelming love. I was going to speak but my thoughts were interrupted by the unknown voice;

"We have not finished, there is one further proof for you."

With that, the circle of light around me expanded inwards and poured into my heart and body. My senses and every cell within me felt as if it would explode in this overwhelming surge of light, which I can only describe as 'liquid love'. My consciousness could barely function, it seemed to be floating on an ocean of divine love.

"Be calm, my son, do not try to contain this."

I did my best to follow his instructions, and in doing so, my body felt as if it had completely dissolved into all I was feeling, and my consciousness pathetically attempted to assimilate and make sense of it all. It was impossible to hold onto it for long, but long enough for it to be indelibly fixed in my consciousness.

"I am so sorry, but it was impossible for me to hold on to this experience. It just seemed too much for me."

"We were aware of your efforts, my son. For those few moments, you were in complete unity with us and the Creator of all life. Now you have your proof."

"Thank you, thank you, but why did I find this so difficult here when I have already experienced being in God's love?"

"The first time you experienced the immensity of the divine, you were only able to assimilate the tiniest fraction of God's love, and that was enough for you. Today you were more present than before and therefore able to understand a little more of what it means to be in at onement with the divine."

Before I could utter another word, they dematerialised into the atmosphere, each of them dissipating into billions of tiny points of light which gradually faded into the darkness.

"Oh no, please don't go. I have so much to ask you."

"You always will have, my son, until you know all there is to know."

"That's not fair. I think you are laughing at me and I only want to learn."

"No, my son, we're not laughing at you, but with you. We sense your desire for knowledge of God and can tell you this; to begin to know God, you must be able to dissolve your mind and heart into the immensity of the infinite presence. Remember also, I am aware of your thoughts, no matter where you are and will answer your questions when they need to be answered."

"Please come back and let me be with you a while longer. I feel so alone without you."

"You do not need us by your side, how can you possibly be alone when you have God all around you?"

"Please forgive my selfish behaviour. I cannot thank you enough for all you have shown me. How can I ever repay you?"

"By being of service to your fellow man. Souls will find you who are honestly seeking eternal truth. Help them to grow by sharing your knowledge and understanding with them and yes, before you ask, we will meet again."

What more is there to say?

Before I could think another thought, I was back in my body, sobbing uncontrollably as wave after wave of emotion flooded every fibre of my being. My rational mind was trying unsuccessfully to understand the impossibility of all that had just happened. I knew I was in bed trying to get to sleep but also knew I had left my body, flown across the continents, and landed on a snowy ledge in my pyjamas. This experience was as real to my consciousness as any everyday chore. Yes, the snow beneath my feet was as vivid an experience as getting into bed. So which is reality, standing in the snow or lying in bed asleep? I was aware of both simultaneously, but my mind couldn't rationalise the fact I could be aware of two places at once, yet this was a fact. So, either both experiences are real, or neither is real, and if the latter is true then I am a figment of my own imagination.

You can see my dilemma!

Understanding More

"There are so many questions. Every time I find an answer to one problem, it seems to open a thousand different areas of enquiry."

"It will always be so."

"This may sound rude after all these months, but are you really there, or just a figment of my imagination?"

"Yes I am really here, and to answer your question logically; if I am a product of your imagination where do the answers to your questions come from? My purpose here is to help you grow spiritually. I have to prove myself to you, so a certain amount of faith is required by you until such time as you can fully trust my judgement. Everything must make sense, for the mysteries of the universe can only be revealed gradually to be understood, not only intellectually, but by the very essence of your being. In other words, you must be able to feel the truth as well."

All I reveal to you is for the sole purpose of helping you to return to the giver of all life. I am not interested in knowledge for knowledge's sake, it must have a direct bearing on your soul evolution. Correct knowledge has a resonance which is accepted by the soul itself. The heart recognises truth even if the ego and intellect do not wish to accept it. Erroneous knowledge may appeal to the ego, but it will not resonate within the centre of your being. You cannot find God in a book. The infinite cannot be contained in the finite, and no pages have ever been written that contain all knowledge of the Creator.

Do not be offended by my words, just go outside and look at the night sky. Then try to find any books containing all the information of every single star that you can see, and what about those yet to be discovered. Returning closer to home, has everything been discovered about the human body and cures for its ailments, and this is just the world you can see. What about the spiritual universe? Has all knowledge been recorded about that? I think not.

To begin the eternal journey of God's understanding, we must be able to feel the Creator's presence. Without this feeling in your heart, it is purely an empty, intellectual exercise with absolutely no expansion of the soul at all.

The greatest prophets ever to incarnate on earth may state 'they are in at onement with the Creator', but none ever say they are the Creator. To put it simply, the child can never be the equal of the spiritual parent. Also, while I am talking of God, God has no gender, so is not an old man with grey hair floating around the universe. In fact, God has no form at all, therefore can only be felt by those willing enough to persevere with their practices and desire to be with the Creator. However, I am not here to debate the inaccuracy of theological texts with you. Do you know there are souls over here who were once scholars on earth, who have spent decades trying to make sense of the dogma of earth's religions, in the hope of finding the key to the gates of heaven?

As if there was a key in the first place!
or even any gates!

So, back to more serious business. The information I will pass on to you was given to me by those great souls whose spiritual attainment is beyond question. I can guarantee this information is correct because of the expansion of my soul as I learnt it. If it were false, there would be no soul growth at all. I am then passing this knowledge to you, allowing you to understand all you have seen, felt and heard. You, in turn, have been asked to write down your experiences by your friends so other sincere souls may grasp some aspects of the reality of eternal existence. So it goes on, generation after generation, sharing the experiences and knowledge we have learnt for the benefit of others.

You asked me some time ago how you would understand, the superficial observation being you would see, hear or feel it. You have already devised a formula for yourself, enabling you to separate fact from fiction, so now I would like to explain the process in more detail.

You are aware that everything in the universe is vibrating at different speeds, including yourself. When you learn something, that knowledge is directed towards you in the form of energy and is absorbed into your consciousness, which vibrates at a certain speed. This is the important part.

Truth vibrates in harmony with the core of your being, meaning, when your consciousness has absorbed true facts, they vibrate in harmony with the soul, thereby energising and expanding it. This is achieved gradually, allowing the individual to adjust to the greater awareness of the truth they have been given. Conversely, incorrect information may be retained intellectually, but will not resonate harmoniously deep within the soul. Therefore, the individual will have no expansion of being, just a consciousness full of inharmonious vibrations.

An analogy is this; truth is like putting pieces of a jigsaw in their correct place, enabling us to see the picture we are creating. Put them in the wrong place and the picture is distorted leading to confusion and frustration.

Looks like I'm going to be doing a lot of jigsaws!

Controversy or Not

"We have talked a lot about the Creator, is there a destroyer or devil? It would be good to know how to deal with it if I bump into one. There's no point living in La La Land."

"Cast your mind back to some of your earlier experiences and our subsequent conversations. Before the universe and all the spiritual dimensions existed, there was only this force (God) everywhere, ready to put all of creation into being. Logically, if the only thing to exist before creation was God, who created the devil—if there is one? Even those darkest places which you have seen were not created by any devil but by the negative actions of many souls over the millennia. God has allowed those places to exist within creation so that mankind may learn the error of his ways. The magnetic pull of their deeds on earth pulls them towards those dark places where they cannot escape until they change their ways. I have made enquiries from many of the greatest souls ever to have existed on earth and they all say the same thing, 'God alone is omnipotent—the devil, as a person, has never existed.'"

"However, they all admit that the collective negativity of mankind is like a spiritual fog that can engulf the world in times of conflict. This fog or energy has no life of its own, but sometimes it can be drawn upon by those with evil intent.

Think of the charismatic rants of some of the most evil dictators and you can get a glimpse of my meaning."

"There are people who say they have seen demons or even the devil himself and would swear on their lives they have spoken to them. This can be explained quite simply. On earth, criminals will often wear grotesque masks when committing a crime to hide their true identity, but we all know this is just a disguise. So it is with these so-called demons or devils. They are merely evil-minded souls trying to intimidate you by imitating something or someone you are afraid of."

"Yes, but they say they will do terrible things to me."

"99% of all these threats made to people are impossible for them to carry out on earth as they do not possess the required energy or knowledge to carry out their threats. I fully understand the fear generated by these souls, but that is exactly what they need to feed on. The individual's own fear!"

People on earth must remember this is **your** dimension, and it is **your** right to be here, given by God. They are the intruders, wandering near the earth plane, lost and with evil intent, looking for souls to terrorise. But, remember this, they are at a great disadvantage, no matter what they say. Earth is not their dimension and they burn up much of their own energy trying to remain nearby. They desperately need a victim's fear to sustain their masquerade until such time as they cry out in remorse for all they have done. Then and only then can they be helped. You cannot assess their remorse while you are on earth, for these souls have lied, cheated and worse while on earth and continued to do so, even after death.

There are people on earth who say they have spiritual guides and helpers to assist these souls onward to the next dimension, and there are some who genuinely do so. But, how many psychics and mediums have actually asked their guides if this is what they want to do? If one of these criminals sincerely asks for help then yes, they will receive it, but they most certainly will not be entering the gates of heaven to the sound of trumpets or anything else. It is the duty of those who answer their call for help to escort them to places befitting the sum total of their actions, and this is something not everyone in our realm is suited to do, either mentally or emotionally. Just as on earth, not everyone is suited to be an officer of the law.

You see, there is a lot to learn.

On the subject of negative forces, please do not be under the illusion that chants, burning herbs, drawing symbols, or waving religious regalia of any kind in the air will protect you from attack. After all, could any of these things prevent a burglar from entering your home? I don't think so. Having said all this, please do not despair, thinking there is no protection against these forces.

That is where you are wrong.

The greatest protection of all is the radiance and strength of your soul as you meditate and align yourself with the Creator. This brightness will shine from your heart, and those positive vibrations will energise the aura which surrounds you, making it so out of alignment with your attacker's energy they will be temporarily blinded if they draw near to you. Also, the strength of this vibration will neutralise any negative energy they may try to hurt you with.

I can give you a simple test to prove the truth of my words.

Go into a darkened room and close the door. The darkness symbolises the negativity of the world and these evil souls. Now, switch on the light. What happens to the darkness? It disappears! You can repeat this test from now until the end of time, the result will always be the same. Light overcomes darkness every time. A rather pessimistic person once said to me, "Yes, and then the darkness always returns," to which I replied—"Then don't switch the light off!"

Find the Creator's light within you and you can never be overcome by the forces of darkness.

Birth

By now, my mind was overloaded with so many spiritual facts, I felt as if it was going to burst. Time to bring myself back to more earthly matters and deal with the facts of life, so I better start at the beginning.

"Can you explain the process of birth to me?"

"Yes, I can, presuming you mean the spiritual process and not the physical one?"

"Sorry, the spiritual process please."

"You know some of these facts will not be to everyone's liking."

"Probably, but facts are facts and it is useful to know them whether we like them or not."

"Very well. Firstly, we will all experience several births on earth in the course of our soul's evolutionary journey, but first birth or last, the spiritual process is the same."

"Any adult on our side of life who wishes to experience an earthly lifetime must begin a nine-month meditation corresponding to the development of the child's body in the womb. The purpose of this meditation is to relegate all memories of life over here, as well as all mental and physical abilities to their subconscious mind, thereby leaving them with a clear and uncluttered consciousness, ready to learn and experience all that life has to offer."

"At the precise moment of fertilisation, the energy in the egg, the sperm and the soul waiting over here combine to initiate the growth process and an energetic cord is formed between them, only to be broken when death occurs. This fine energetic cord, called the astral cord, then strengthens throughout the duration of the pregnancy."

"Many people believe the soul enters the egg at the moment of fertilisation, but this is untrue. Yes, there is an energetic union between the two, as I said earlier, but not a complete entry of the soul into the egg. It is only at the precise moment of birth that the waiting soul fully enters the child's body. Before that time, the soul in deep meditation is able to move the baby's limb in the womb by thought process travelling along the astral cord and into the baby's body. Then when the moment of birth arrives, the contractions in the mother's body are the signal for the waiting soul to enter the child as the astral cord tightens thereby securing the owner with its new body and the baby is born ready to begin life on earth."

Rebirth

"Now I have given you a brief summary of the process of the soul's entry into the child's body upon birth, does it seem logical, given the vastness and diversity of life on earth, that we are given only one lifetime to experience it all?"

"Or, from a religious viewpoint, one lifetime to get everything right or be condemned to an eternity of some kind of hell. Just as a wise parent helps their children to learn and give them another chance, so from the perspective of a succession of lives on earth, we are given more chances to attune ourselves to the Creator by right actions and thereby move to a better state of existence."

"Why would people want to come back to earth when they could learn in your dimension?"

"Firstly, wrong actions on earth can only be rectified when back on earth because the energetic and magnetic pull brings you back and prevents you from moving forward until all is balanced and correct in this respect. If you make a mess in the kitchen, you have to return to clean it up. Secondly, it can take much longer to change oneself over here because there isn't the urgency to do so compared to the need to achieve a change in one's lifetime before one dies."

"There are many reasons why souls wish to return to earth, sometimes it can be a desire to be of service to mankind, in whichever way possible, medicine, science, teaching or a spiritual quest. This is hard-wired into their subconscious mind before birth, and fulfilment for them comes only from the pursuit of these desires."

"There is usually a lengthy period of time before one can be reborn on earth, ranging from at least one hundred years to maybe a thousand or so depending on the individual circumstances. So, although one may have karma to atone for, and earthly desires to fulfil, one must learn to overcome the urges that caused the negative impulses in the first place. Otherwise, you can add to earthly karma instead of repaying it, by getting things wrong when one returns to earth once more."

"To summarise my conversation with you; science is completely unable to either prove or disprove the case for multiple lives on Earth, so cannot help here at all. Religions are also conflicted, with some firmly stating the case for one life while others advocate many, and neither being able to prove their statements or disprove the opposite."

"The reason this problem has intrigued mankind for millennia, without being resolved to universal satisfaction, is this; all memory of life before birth is incapsulated in the subconscious mind allowing for a complete blank canvas of consciousness for the infant. Unfortunately, this leads many to believe that because they cannot remember anything before their birth, then it did not exist. So, the statement 'if I can't remember it then it didn't happen,' sounds a little unconvincing."

Destiny

"So, I have spoken briefly of the process of birth and how the soul enters the child's body. This is only the start of the story. You are aware on earth of the genetic make-up of a baby's body as being a composite of the parents' DNA. As you are discovering, many physical weaknesses can be detected through the examination of the genetic code and many more will be discovered in the coming years. But there is also the spiritual DNA, which is the individual's mental and emotional make-up, otherwise known as their karma. Many people on earth do not believe in karma, probably hoping that if they say it often enough it won't apply to them! However, there is one irrefutable test to prove the law of cause and effect (karma)."

"If you hit yourself on the head with a hammer, it will hurt—a lot. You are the cause and you suffer the effect. If you do it again—it will hurt even more. You can repeat this as often as you wish, the outcome will always be the same—pain until you stop doing it. This is how we learn from our errors in judgment. They will always cause us pain, either mental, physical, emotional, or a combination of them all until we learn not to repeat our mistakes."

"There is one obvious example of karma which no one can dispute. If you are born on this earth, you will die, nobody gets out alive. You can be as philosophical or as mentally convoluted as you wish, even arguing these points for years until—yes you've guessed it—you die!"

"Now, just so you don't think that is all there is to it, I need to say you also have free will. Well, you might ask, how does that fit in with the law of karma? It does, and I will try to simplify this as much as possible, Firstly, you have your own free will to stop hitting yourself on the head."

"Yes, but if it is my karma to hit myself on the head, surely I can't avoid it?"

"Correct, if that was the lesson you had to learn. But, having hit yourself and experienced the pain it caused, hopefully, you learnt the karmic lesson from it and so were free from repeating the actions over and over again until you did learn. Hence the interaction of karma and free will to learn life's lessons."

Before anyone arrives on earth, they calculate how much of their previous negative karma, if they had any, they could conceivably make amends for in the forthcoming life. These points are usually significant milestones for them to encounter and hopefully react to in the best way possible. Unfortunately, this does not always happen, and people do not rise to the challenges they have set for themselves. If that is the case, then at the end of their earthly life, they look back at the opportunities and situations they missed and deeply regret their actions. This leads to another return to earth to rectify these wrongdoings and so eventually free themselves from the ties of earthly karma. As you can see, nothing is truly set in stone as a certainty until it becomes the past. All of us, no matter which dimension we live in, can only live in the present moment. Our actions in the present set the unalterable past and our desires lead us to our future potential.

A little more about karma. Not all karma is negative; it can also be positive, in which we reap the rewards of past good deeds. These 'gifts of good fortune' are bonuses in our daily lives and should serve as a platform for further acts of kindness in the future. Conversely, negative karma has a limiting effect on our lives due to the trauma of experiencing the negative consequences of our past actions. This in turn will hopefully prevent reoffending in the future and thus, of our own free will, we then create good karma instead of bad.

Some more on free will. Why would anyone make bad decisions when they can make good ones? The answer lies in their motives for doing so. Anger, greed, cruelty and deceit are just some of the overriding emotions that cause people to make errors in judgement and then suffer the consequences of their actions in this life or the next. For them to try to absolve themselves of any kind of responsibility, by pleading ignorance of the right course of action to follow, is absolute rubbish. Every person born on earth comes from the same creative life force and therefore every person has a conscience, which is a fundamental part of our subconscious mind. So even the most evil of souls knows the difference between right and wrong, they just refuse to pay attention to it. But, no matter which dimension they reside in, and no matter how hard they try to obliterate it, their conscience will always make itself heard.

Think of this also; any thought or action, if repeated often enough, becomes engrained in a person's consciousness. In other words, a strong energetic or neural connection is formed. Whether it is good or bad it doesn't matter, the process is the same. Therefore, it is only common sense to see that any habits and neural connections, we create can also be uncreated. To those who say they cannot give something up because they have an addictive personality, I say this, "Whatever you start, you can stop. Do not use your addictive personality as a reason to continue your old habits. Use it to become addicted to God instead, for only the knowledge that God is within you, and being able to feel God within you, will bring lasting peace and contentment."

As you can see from these few basic examples, everyone has a destiny to fulfil but not everyone does so fully, for there are no guarantees one way or another. Criteria that should be met are not, desires that could be overcome are more deeply entrenched. Yet for others, their life on earth becomes a triumph over adversity. Through sheer strength of purpose and resolve, they harness their free will to defeat everything negative they are faced with. They never complain or say 'why me' and are more than grateful for all they are given, treating it as a blessing from God. These people are the true saints on earth, you would walk past them in the street not knowing the spiritual strength they possess.

Kind, unassuming, gentle and full of love—true role models for all to behold.

Communication

"The purpose of life on earth is to allow each individual to express their hopes and dreams, desires and destiny, love and loneliness, joy and sorrow and everything in between. With all of this filling our waking hours, most people have no knowledge or interest in spiritual matters until something goes wrong."

"Then, for some, a search for a psychic or clairvoyant is a way of hopefully finding the right answers to their problems. If the psychic is honest, they have a spiritual duty to offer their services in as clear and concise a way as possible, without any vagaries or guesswork to justify their fee. The availability of so much psychic information from the internet is a two-edged sword, truth is being written, but there is also so much outrageous and meaningless rubbish which can leave the individual confused and in despair. It can be so hard to distinguish fact from fiction, but this is nothing new. Unfortunately, it has always been so."

"We over here know that the best psychics and clairvoyants are born for that purpose, but even they must learn to use their gifts wisely, otherwise they will diminish and their health can be affected adversely."

"You cannot learn to be a medium on a weekend course—or any course at all—no matter who runs it or how much they charge. It is a gift you are born with and it requires a lifetime of discipline, dedication, practice and humility to the giver of all life. Psychic abilities should not be used to inflate the medium's ego nor to amass fame and fortune, but should be used in the service of humanity to alleviate suffering and despair."

What Are We?

I woke very early one morning—3 am—with a thought on my mind which wouldn't go away, *What am I?*

I know I have experienced many wonderful things, and at times, felt I didn't know who or what I was, but I would always revert back to being me after a while, although strictly that statement isn't accurate. No one can experience all I have, physically or mentally, without it having some effect on one's outlook, so I decided to analyse not only what I am, but who I am and maybe that will give me an understanding of all of us.

I thought the best way to approach this was to leave my body and observe me 'the person' without identifying myself with my physical form.

So, standing beside my bed looking at the flesh and bones I call 'me', it was easy to understand the first part of this process that I am more than just a body composed of trillions of cells pulsating with energy.

So far so good.

Next, I looked at the body I was inhabiting. Well, it looked the same as the one in the bed and yet it wasn't. Although visually it replicated that body, it had a vibrancy and weightlessness about it that a physical body could never have. It looked more or less the same, perhaps a little younger, but it was definitely more 'alive and responsive'. What I could do was look at it closely, as if through a microscope. There were no atoms or molecules or anything resembling the composition of our physical frame at all, except one thing, a pulsating energy. So my physical body and my spiritual body were both composed of energy, the exact same energy, just moulded differently.

What about my personality and what is 'me'? I know every thought is energy and there is a corresponding energy charge in the brain. I also understand some thoughts generate an emotional response, which is also energy. I understand thoughts and emotions are perceived by us merely because they have come within our area of experience thus far and this, coupled with an identification with our physical body, begins to give us a semblance of individuality and identity. But there is more than this relatively superficial level of experience. The more profound emotions of love, hate, fear, laughter, etc., I feel on a deeper level of experience within me and seem to make up the core of my being. But, when I looked within myself, I realised they were not in the centre of me but around me.

The deepest part of my being is not within my consciousness, but within my soul, or to put it another way, the point of emergence of my life force lies within my heart. My consciousness identifies the fact that there is a point within my body and being that radiates energy towards my bodily functions, senses, thoughts and emotions.

Everything about 'me' my body, mind, senses and emotions, I am easily able to say are 'mine'. But when I look at the point of origin within, I cannot say it is 'mine'. I know it is there, but I do not 'possess' it, nor can I quantify it in any way, shape or form. When I delve deep into its presence, it expands outwards in all directions towards infinity, enabling me to 'feel' my life force is part of the infinite life force which men call God.

So, what are we?

Well, put simply, we are points of the infinite life force encased in a physical body with the ability to think and sense the universe around us coupled with a burning curiosity to discover and understand all there is, and ultimately be in 'at onement' with the essence of our being.

This is us—humanity—all of us, struggling to understand who we are and the meaning of our existence. We are just bundles of energy in an energetic universe that is constantly changing. Nothing is permanent; only the energy itself, which men call God.

Looking at this fact from a purely mental level, it seems cold, hard, bleak and almost depressing in its finality, but if you add the emotional facts to this statement, suddenly everything changes. Whether you like it or not, we are all emotional beings (some definitely more emotional than others). We cannot totally suppress or eradicate our emotional make-up, nor should we. It is our emotions that bring colour to the stark reality of existence.

Religion

When I was young, I was told never to discuss politics or religion with people because they can be very contentious issues, but having written about so many controversial topics already I don't think one more will do any harm. Looking back over the course of human history, from time to time souls have been born on earth whose words and deeds have comforted and inspired many millions of people. The details of their lives and the recording of their discourses have given many hope, encouragement and a sense of purpose to deal with life's problems.

Upon analysis, their messages were all basically the same, that life continues after death, there is a greater power, do good to others, etc. They wanted mankind to follow their examples, to try to understand what they intuitively understood. These are noble intentions indeed.

However, humanity being what it is, began to misinterpret what seemed to be fairly straightforward advice on how to live into various sects, splits and branches, with each claiming the exclusive right to the 'true understanding' of the prophets' words.

Wars ensued.

So, does ending the life of someone with a different idea of heaven to you make your beliefs more valid? What gives anyone the right to kill in God's name when God created us all in the first place? All the great prophets speak of God as the Creator of all life, so it is not their fault that so much bloodshed and destruction has happened, but the fault of some of those who profess to follow them.

That is the negative side of religion, the positive side is the overwhelming evidence of good that has been done in their name; charities, institutions and people devoting their whole lives for the good of others, inspired by the lives of those great souls who have gone before them. Music, art and architecture have all found their inspiration in the worship of the Creator, and through their awe-inspiring beauty, countless others have been spiritually inspired to do good works.

Worship is only part of the story. To praise God in prayer and music does uplift the soul, but that is not enough. We must strive, wherever possible, to be of service to our fellow man. If each of us merely takes from the world instead of giving as well, there will be nothing left for future generations. That is simply mathematics. Possessions do not make us lead better or longer lives but can make us possessive, mean and insecure. Money itself is neither good nor bad, it is our attitude towards it that is the problem.

The prophets advocated a simple way of life as the best way to draw closer to God. That means being financially independent where possible, a good friend and neighbour, an honest employer or employee, instilling wholesome values in one's family and oneself and having time for contemplation, prayer or meditation, as well as fun. It is not such an impossible task in today's world as one would think, after all, try to imagine how those great souls would advise us if they were born on earth today.

Whatever you feel their advice would be, it most certainly would not be to kill others in God's name for:

God is the only Creator of all life on earth!

Consciousness

Isn't it strange how things come into your mind while you are doing mundane chores—well, they certainly do to me. I was mowing the lawn on a beautiful May afternoon, and the word **consciousness** rang loud and clear in my thoughts.

"That's interesting, I didn't expect that."

The idea of writing about consciousness seemed quite uplifting for a few moments, until the reality of the challenge sank in, for I instinctively knew that it wasn't so much about how the consciousness works, but about what the consciousness is!

So, let's start with the Oxford Dictionary definition of the word conscious: A state of being aware.

Well, that helped a bit, but it didn't say what it was—being aware is what it does. We could study the function of the brain but no matter how much depth we go into, it will only give us part of the story because our physical brain is just the mechanism which translates the information while we are in our body. It has nothing to do with our conscious self when we are asleep, under anaesthetic, in a coma or outside our body. All of these states of un-consciousness are merely the brain not receiving external information and being able to transmit it to the consciousness, and vice-versa.

For days and weeks, random thoughts came into my mind and were quickly dismissed as being mere functions of the consciousness—nothing came close to helping me understand the source or composition of it. To say I felt frustrated is nothing short of a major understatement and no matter how much I pleaded for help, none came. Perhaps I'll try asking in a different way, in fact, as many different ways as I can think of—nothing worked. Eventually, I realised that I had to work it out myself and not just expect the answer to appear, just because I asked. I have been given so much already and it is obviously up to me to use this knowledge and find the answer, so here we go.

I have found there are two main approaches to understanding consciousness:

1. The scientific way
2. The religious way

So, I will begin with the scientific:

Science says the energy of the universe is continually recycling itself from gases into galaxies and back again. We too have come into being from this same energy source—except we call it evolution. Therefore, consciousness must derive from the energy of the universe because logically, there just isn't anything else. Our identity is centred around the nucleus of experiences and ideas gathered from the moment we are born until we die. Put simply, consciousness in us and in all living things is animate energy, while the stuff of the universe is inanimate energy—just as ice, water and steam are all manifestations of H_2O. So, the power source of the universe is the same power source of our consciousness, but unfortunately, our innate sense of self-identity leads us to erroneously think otherwise.

I know these sweeping statements may seem outrageous to many, but what other conclusions can we come to?

There is only so much energy in the universe, no more has been created since the beginning of time, therefore everything in the physical universe—seen and unseen—is created from the same 'stuff'—including us. We were neither created, nor have we evolved from something else, or from some other place. So, we—mind (consciousness), body and spirit (like it or not) are definitely a living part of all there is.

If we now conduct this investigation from a religious viewpoint, we are created in God's image, from the essence of God within God's creation. Therefore, our consciousness contains a living spark of divine energy. This does not mean we are God—just as a spark is not the whole fire, but is created from, and is part of, the flame. So, to stop any grandiose ideas that we may be God himself, we are surrounded by many, many layers of energy—rather like an onion. These have the purpose of giving us an identity, an idea of self, and being the repository of every thought and emotion since birth. Each experience is a thin shell of energy encapsulating our conscious self and held in place by the magnetic vibrations of our aura. These layers, coupled with the inevitable ageing and frailty of the human form, further enhance the sense of individuality keeping us 'grounded' intellectually. It is only when we wish to understand ourselves and search for a meaning to existence, or even a Creator, that the inward search begins.

Why inward? Well, if we look outward at the universe, all we see are the physical manifestations of God's creation;

galaxies, stars and planets etc. To find God, the Creator of consciousness, the only other place left to look is inward. But first, we need to face all the layers of self and truly understand them for what they are—and believe me, this is not a five-minute job! Just think, when you have dealt with everything else within yourself, what is left, but the origin of your soul and consciousness. At first, it seems to be a place of apparent 'nothingness', but there is no such thing; it just takes a while to adjust to the stillness, peace and serenity because at that moment we are using our sixth sense. Everyone has a sixth sense—despite many denying its existence and most being unaware of how to use it. Some call it intuition, and on a superficial level it can manifest that way in our daily lives, but the true purpose, in my opinion, is to find God.

Our physical senses: taste, touch, sight, sound and smell are projected outwards to help us navigate our way through the material world and we need our intellect to decipher and recognise them for what they are. Prayer and meditation help us to switch off from the material world and then our intellect and our sixth sense help us to experience inwardly the vibrancy of the Divine Creator. This is 'the peace of God which passes all understanding'. How can I say that? Because there is nothing else. There are no barriers at all when you reach this point, whichever way you look—up, down, forward, back, left or right—there is a seamless flow of the Divine Consciousness, and we are living within that. We are not observing or experiencing this from 'some other place' for it flows right through us, making us a seamless part of the infinite, only held in place by our perception of self-identity, rather like the raindrops within the ocean.

But, the real truth is all consciousness belongs to God. And we only experience an infinitesimally small part of it.

Grief

If you have been fortunate enough to love someone, it may be that on some terrible day in the future you will lose them. Whether it is sudden or expected, your world will be overturned. You may feel shattered, exhausted, numb, hysterical or hollow. However you feel—life will never be the same. It cannot be—for they are no longer here. No matter what anyone says to the contrary—that part of your life is over and will never return.

If you are going through this—or have gone through it—there are many good books to help you deal with the loss. However, I wish to help you understand, from our perspective over here the emotional spiritual and mechanical process of this traumatic event.

If you have read this book so far, hopefully, it has given you an understanding of what happens to the person you have lost. Their pain and suffering have gone, and they are restored to their healthy former self. They have no worries except for you and the grief you are experiencing. They will want to let you know they are well, and not to worry—but that isn't always possible straight away. First, they must learn to focus all their attention on you and then with the same focus will think their message to you. Obviously, it's no good for them to shout because you wouldn't be able to hear them, so they must learn to think their message instead. Secondly, and probably more importantly, you must learn to listen—not with your ears, but with your mind.

It is not easy for me to say this—but there is so much that has to be right before this can happen.

You have just suffered a tremendous shock and your consciousness will be anything other than calm. The life you created together is in tatters and you need to slowly salvage what you can.

To look at it spiritually; when you love someone, there is a harmonious synchronisation of vibrations from one heart to the other. This creates a strong energetic bond which is then added to with all the things you have shared, large or small, in your time together. These are added energetic ties in your memory and in your heart, which are magnified by your mutual love, respect and recognition, each for the other.

Suddenly the focus of all this love and energy is gone—it feels as if all the ties have been broken and they are no longer here to fill your soul with love as they always used to. You feel empty and hollow.

Fear not.

I cannot bring them back to you, but I can help you understand how to feel their love once more. It will not be as it was, but a more refined and purified form of all you once shared.

You need time. You cannot rush this; your mind and soul need time to adjust. There will be much to do physically to sort everything out, and after all the initial sympathy from everyone, they too have their lives to lead, and you will be alone.

This is when your soul truly begins to settle into your new life. New routines will begin, but they are just for you, rather than shared, so they will never feel the same. However, remember this—from the moment they died and joined us over here, their love for you remained the same. All through those days, weeks and months, they never stopped loving you. You just could not feel it in the shock and turmoil of it all. But now, although life is a little calmer, there are waves of grief to deal with. They well up from the centre of your being like a volcano of emotion, uncontrollable at times, prolonged at others. In your moments alone, never be afraid to let the emotion out. You have been like a pressure cooker with the lid firmly fixed on. Now, in your solitude, take the lid off and empty your soul of this unwanted emotion, for underneath this excruciating emotional pain is the love you always shared, waiting silently for you to rediscover it.

Remember, this grief can only match the love you feel for each other; it can never exceed it. So that means one day all the grief will have been cried out of your soul and you will be able to recall everything about them without that stabbing in your heart because only the love will remain.

"How can that be? They are still not here."

Physically, yes, they have gone but this grief is also the emotional manifestation of the trauma and all the unfulfilled dreams and aspirations you might have shared. After all, your love was both physical and spiritual and you are learning to make the adjustment to spiritual only.

There comes a pivotal point in all of this when the individual must choose which path to travel on, and the choice is this:

1. You can choose to believe their life ended with the last breath on earth and they no longer exist. Then, the possibilities of your consciousness and soul being in harmony with your beloved will be closed down, rather similar to those times on earth if you had an argument the harmonious flow of emotion was abruptly and temporarily terminated! Then your beloved will have to wait silently for your own demise, and you will see they did exist after all!
2. If you believe in the possibility of the continuation of your beloved's life after death, even though you don't know how or where, your consciousness and soul retain a semblance of the fluidity of thought and emotion that you used to share. We can see this from over here, your consciousness radiates what can best be described as an anticipatory longing towards your beloved. This means the only barrier between the two of you is that one of you has a body on earth and the other has a body over here and you both need to learn how to communicate.

As I said earlier, I cannot bring them back to you physically, but I can give you the knowledge and tools to help you feel their love for you.

So, we must begin with you practising the mediation exercise written about earlier in this book. This will have the effect of calming your mind and soul so you may hear or feel the communication from your partner.

They, over here, must learn to project their thoughts to a specific point—you—so you can receive them. To put it another way—you are learning to recognise and receive their energy waves and they are learning to project their energy to you.

In a nutshell, that is it!

Time, space and different dimensions do not matter in this process, because the magnetic pull from the heart chakra—each to the other, eventually overcomes all obstacles! For deep within the heart is where God resides, so God is pulling God towards him, or to put it another way, love within is pulling the love towards it.

So, having learnt to quieten yourself, rather similar to the way you do before falling asleep, you must then wait for them to speak to you. When you first hear their voice, it probably will not be with your ears, but it will be within you. You will 'hear' their voice within your head and consciousness and probably think you are making it up. We certainly want you to keep your powers of reason and discernment, so, here is a good test:

If you ever feel you are creating the dialogue—that may be happening. See if you can create it exactly as you heard it and I mean exactly, with the exact same sound of their voice—not an approximation. If you can, then you were making it up—if you cannot recreate it exactly, then it wasn't you. This simple test will help you not to fool yourself. after all, we are searching for truth here—not illusion.

That is how you start a dialogue between yourselves, and if your beloved is determined and focused enough then maybe one day, you might be able to feel them near you as well. But that is a conversation between us and them. It is our job to help you to listen, it is your job to practice.

Be patient.

Life

What is it?

And more importantly—how do we understand it?

The only way we can analyse life itself is through introspection and meditation.

Why meditation? Because it helps us disassociate ourselves from the thoughts and emotions in our daily lives and to become aware of the inner stillness.

Why is that important? Because we have to be able to feel our life before we can begin to understand it. Then, we can use our own intelligence and powers of logic and reason to delve further.

If we use logic, we must start at the beginning before even the universe came into being. The only thing that existed before creation was the stillness, therefore, logic dictates that all the known universe came into being from within the stillness and this means that all things contain the stillness, including us!

Science, so far, says everything comes from something—so, whichever form of creation you believe in, everything has come from the same place. To go one step further, all the ingredients for life have come from the stillness. We know what the components are for physical life, yet we cannot replicate life ourselves.

We cannot create life.

Neither can we go to a chemist and buy a bottle of 'life.'

So, what is life, and where does it come from?

Life itself has not been created or evolved from the stuff of the universe. If it had, we would be able to manufacture it ourselves from the very material at our disposal. Therefore, the only place it could come from is the stillness before creation. Again, as nothing can come from nothing, life had to be in the uncreated absolute before the universe existed. So, this life within you, and also all living things, was around before creation and within the stillness.

How? I don't know.

Why? I don't know.

All we can be certain of, is that life is within us and we exist. Life itself is as it always was and as I said before, it has not evolved. Our understanding of it, and the way it manifests on earth has evolved, but life itself remains the same.

In other words, you are either alive or you are not!

So, this life within us is more than our thoughts, emotions and awareness for it sustains them all.

We carry on our daily existence totally unaware of the underlying life force. Even when we die it is still there—it just transfers itself from our physical body and takes us with it.

I personally can vouch for that.

Just stop for a moment and try to be aware of the life within you, for it will be the same when you leave this earth. You will be as you always have been for the life force cannot be destroyed. It will sustain you for all eternity while you experience all things. Your consciousness will become aware of it, your emotions will respond to it and you will slowly realise that it silently draws you towards itself. There is an irresistible pull—almost imperceptible at first—that encourages you to explore further and 'be at one' with it.

Why? You may well ask.

What is the purpose of being drawn towards an infinite nothingness? I cannot say what the purpose is, other than the incredible feeling of freedom from the constraints of our mental, emotional and physical boundaries. Why would any of us wish to be contained by anything when we can be free to explore everything?

Which brings me to the next question: Why were we bound by these so-called barriers in the first place? I am not sure. I can only speak from my own experiences, and I know that I had to assimilate all of them slowly. It would have been too much for me to grasp the immensity of space and the things beyond this physical universe in one brief moment.

To understand them intellectually was difficult enough, but to feel the energy within all things made me feel as if I was going to explode.

Perhaps someone more spiritually aware than I would have been better able to cope.

At times, I felt like a raindrop, overwhelmed by a billion vast oceans, and even that is a poor analogy, but I think you may understand my meaning.

So, to return to the beginning and understand that meditation reinforces our awareness of life itself, we begin to perceive that the life force is in all things. As I said before, life must have existed 'before' creation and then manifested itself 'within' creation, and as creation evolved into mankind, there arose a need to understand and revere the unknown. Firstly, in the worship of nature and the seasons and then the creative force 'behind' nature, and so eventually, the concept of a 'benevolent being' overseeing creation was born.

Mankind intuitively felt there was a force greater than himself, and some felt the need to draw closer to that force and understand and worship it as 'sacred'. So, the word 'God' came into being, and ever since then, successive generations have tried to understand what the previous ones have been talking about!

We each have our allotted time on earth and then we leave. No one remains here forever, and it is only when we can perceive infinity and all there is for the first time, that our eyes are truly opened. While we are on earth, none of us can possibly grasp the immensity of creation or the life force within it.

So, I put this to you:

That it is this 'life force' within 'all things' that men have called 'God'.

For those who are of a religious disposition—of which I am one in my own way—please do not dismiss my words without reading further. For when I say 'God' is the 'Life force' of the universe, that is in no way a disparaging statement. Quite the opposite. It is an acknowledgement that life itself is the most precious thing that we possess—for obviously, without it we would not even exist!

So, when we are faced with death—we cling to life. Everything else pales into insignificance; no longer do we crave money, fame or power, our sole focus is only to live.

With this, ultimate experience ahead of us we suddenly become aware of how much:

> We love life
> We are desperate for life
> We crave life
> We cling to life

Now I will change the word 'life' to God:

> We love God
> We are desperate for God
> We crave God
> We cling to God

You see how in the hour of our need, the two are indivisible. There will be those who wholeheartedly agree with the first statements but perhaps hesitate in their acknowledgement of the latter. I personally feel this is not entirely the individual's fault, but more of an indication of the collective awareness of mankind and society in general.

For you cannot have life without God within it.
They are not two separate entities…

They are one.

Reflections

Some friends asked me, "What have you learnt from all that has happened?" It made me stop and think and try to look at myself as honestly as I could, which is quite a difficult thing to do under any circumstances.

Firstly, I am still me, despite all the incredible experiences, good and bad, amazing and unbelievable, I am fundamentally the same person. What has happened is I don't worry about anything anymore. All the times I have left my body in meditation have shown me that I can and do exist without it. It has the sensation of just being an overcoat I put on to communicate with my friends and the world in general (although, as overcoats go I'm looking a bit old and tatty now!).

Looking outward helped me to understand a little about the universe, but it did not give me an understanding of myself or my motives, how I exist or why. That was only done by looking inward.

Looking beneath my thoughts and emotions is not always easy, but possible for all who are searching. I understood they were merely different vibrational energies in my consciousness and energy field. Most of us become enmeshed in their impact on our being, but if we learn to see them for what they are and feel beneath all this turmoil, then we come to a place of stillness and peace. Not a nothingness, but an unquantifiable and yet intangible feeling, unlike any emotion we may experience on earth. It is neither empty nor hollow but possesses an immovable energy that sustains us through the ups and downs of our journey through life.

This is one of the most important lessons of all the discoveries I have made. This inner stillness is within all of us, not just me, but you as well. It is our connection to the life force of the universe and beyond.

Without it, we cannot even exist.

Our awareness of the universe is limited by our five senses and intellectual ability to process this information. There is much more to existence if we learn to sink into the stillness within and allow it to show us the unseen and unknowable.

On a more personal level and I include all humanity in this, we do not become ghostlike when we die. We retain the same solidity over there as we do here, except here our body feels heavy and will age and perhaps become unwell before we die. But there, while our body retains a solidity, it is not full of heart, lungs, stomach etc, but an energy that radiates from the centre of our being and is moulded by the memory of how we looked while on earth. It is this energy that negates the need for internal organs, as on earth, for it truly sustains our whole being with life. No aches and pains, illness or infirmity, but a vibrant form that is full of life.

When souls understand this is the only thing sustaining them for all eternity, they soon forget about eating, sleeping and the need to breathe. They are liberated from the daily chores of maintaining an earthly body and slowly begin to lose awareness of their form. This aids the individual on the slow spiritual climb towards enlightenment. Without a conscious decision to begin the journey of introspection and assimilate the truth of existence in all its forms, it can take an individual many tens of thousands of years (in earth time) to attain any degree of spiritual advancement at all.

There is always freedom of choice over there, to improve oneself or not. It is up to you and you alone. Some choose merely to observe all the universe has to offer. If one has learnt how, even the past can be observed because everything, and I mean everything, since the dawn of creation has left an energy blueprint in eternity that will never be lost.

In merely observing the universe and not engaging with it, an individual can amass vast amounts of knowledge on myriads of subjects but attain no spiritual awareness. This can only be gained through contemplation of one's relationship with infinity and becoming aware of the unity with the self and the Creator.

I have found the laws of creation are exact and unchanging. They have existed since the dawn of time and will continue unchanged until times end. They cannot be altered to suit our limited understanding nor our ego, for they hold the very fabric of creation together.

Ignorance of divine law is ignorance of the divine self, for we are as much a part of creation as anything else and not exempt from it. This is as fundamental as $1+1=2$ This also will never change, neither is it open to interpretation.

There is no chaos, that is a misconception. If one is able to view all creation from the Creator's viewpoint, there is order in all things, from the creation and destruction of galaxies to the death of an ant, everything is merely changing its vibrational frequency, and that energy can be used over and over again in different forms.

Ever-changing patterns of texture, light and life underpinned by the universal laws of existence.

When I first began this journey, my understanding fluctuated wildly between being:

- Emotional-thinking about love
- Mathematical-thinking about balance and numbers
- Religious-thinking about God, and
- Physics-thinking about galaxies and numbers

Each avenue of knowledge is true, but none is the whole truth, they are all aspects of truth leading to the ultimate destination. Just as our arms and legs are not the whole of us, but parts that make up the whole.

Slowly and gradually, these seemingly incompatible truths began to reveal their underlying unity, and each helped me to understand the others in some small way. I say small way for I am no genius, but I suppose I do have a basic grasp of all these different subjects (with physics being my least favourite at school!) However, the search for an understanding of life is not dependent on possessing a massive IQ. One must be able to sense truth as well, and thankfully I have always been able to sense things from an early age. I just had to learn what I was doing, and how to use it.

If you are still reading, I feel I must recount what I have seen and understood about creation and the start of the universe. Much of my experience of this event is contrary to the accepted theory of the 'Big Bang'—which was not even thought of when I was a youngster.

As I was able to look back further and further in time, creation did not emerge from one spot, neither was there an immense explosion creating everything.

I cannot prove this, but I know in a few years hence the scientific establishment will begin to adjust its theories to a less dramatic beginning to all there is.

For the moment, here is my, as yet, unprovable account of the beginning of creation.

Before anything existed, the universe was not dark, neither was it light in the sense that we know it. Nor did time exist, for there were no markers or changes to assess time by.

I tried to look back before the light existed—but there was always a faint glow, nothing before it. Then over what must have been billions of years, the light began to move, not in a sudden violent and explosive way, but as an imperceptibly subtle pulse which gathered momentum over the aeons. This change wasn't limited to one place in the universe but to many places—not one big bang, but many, many beginnings of the subtlest movements, each independent of the other.

The pulsation and swirling increased in intensity for billions of years leading to the condensation of light into heat and the subsequent process of creation as science now accepts and understands it. As I stated earlier, I do not possess the intellect to express this process scientifically nor am I sufficiently religious to explain it in dogmatic language of any religion.

But I cannot deny, nor can logic dismiss, the facts as I witnessed them. I am not delusional, and I debated with myself whether to include these paragraphs or not. But I have, and it is for you to make up your own mind until you are able to see for yourself the truth of my words when you arrive on the other side of life.

Finally

Many people have asked me, "If there is a God, why does he let us suffer and die and why do we have to lose our partner and be on our own?"

I suppose I can answer both of these questions with a relative amount of experience. Firstly, I can absolutely guarantee there is a continuation of life after we die because having died twice, I have seen and experienced that life goes on. For those who have difficulty accepting my assurances, let us wait until both our lives are over and we can meet over there and I will show you it is all true.

Remember, the physical universe is the only level of existence that requires our death in order for us to move on, and the only one where we die without knowing what comes next.

All other transitions from the astral level to the causal require that we merely allow our form to dissolve into light, as opposed to leaving it behind as we do on Earth. Then comes the ultimate change when our form dissolves in its entirety and forever to allow us to fully become in atonement with infinite and everlasting bliss.

You may wonder why different realms exist anyway, but it seemed to me that each level was like a classroom and just as children grow and move to higher classes, so as we grow spiritually we go to better realms.

"Why can't we just be created perfect and know everything?" If we knew everything straight away what would be left to discover, what would we do for all eternity if everything was the best it could possibly be without our input? There is a clue in nature. Nothing is fully finished in the plant or animal kingdom when it is born, everything grows and evolves in its own particular way, as do we, which leads to the conclusion we are merely part of creation, not the reason for creation. This fact helps us lose any sense of ego and entitlement and thus begin to feel in harmony with all there is.

I know I have visited other levels and seen how people live, but only after I had died and come back again. I can only assume my earthly life has continued so I may share my experiences for others' benefit. I see no other reason for me surviving all I have.

As for the question, "Why do our loved ones have to die and leave us alone?" From my own experience, I can say this. My partner and I had twenty-five wonderful years together and even though he spent the last ten of those years having strokes, heart attacks, operations, cancer and dialysis, he never once complained, and it was an honour and privilege to look after him.

All through that time I worried for his health, about his suffering, and whether I was a good enough carer to deal with his physical disabilities. Not to mention how I would cope with his death and what I would do with myself after he had gone.

The reason for my telling you is this, even though he was everything I could wish for in a partner, what we shared was tainted by my own fears and the thought of losing him and being alone.

But in the 23 years since his death, I can tell you our love has not diminished at all; in fact, it is a thousand times stronger than it ever was while he was on earth with me.

All I worried about while he was ill has gone, because I know his suffering ceased the moment he drew his last breath. My fear of him dying and our love ending has gone because I know he is with me at all times, not standing by my side for 23 years doing nothing, but in the fact that the effortless flow of my heart's emotions to his, and his to mine, was not severed when he died.

I love him more now than I ever thought possible for nothing, not even his death, has come between, or broken, that which we always had.

So, what do I have and what have I learnt in these 23 years?

Without his death, I would still be full of fears and worries. Without losing him physically, I would still have a deep-seated dread that death would alter or end our love.

But no, It hasn't.

I learnt to understand and overcome grief. I let go of the worries and fears and am left with the vibrant purity and enormity of his love for me. This is not wishful thinking on my part, but a solid emotional presence within the centre of my being which I can feel at all times.

I know he still loves me
For I know I can feel his love for me as I always did

I know it will last for all eternity
I know he is full of the Creator's love
I know I will share that fully with him when I finally leave this earth

Until that time, I will daily strive to do what he asked of me before he died, which was:

'Make me proud of you.'

Epilogue

So, you have made it to the end of this book without throwing it away. Congratulations and thank you.

My motives were only to share what I have seen, felt and heard in the hope you may find answers to your questions and peace in your heart.

Nothing has been written with the intention to upset or offend, only to enlighten and comfort.

My wish is that you find love in your life ahead. Mine is nearing its end—if I haven't gone already—so there probably won't be enough time to have discussions here on Earth on all I have written.

However

Eternity is a long time so when it is your time to arrive on the other side, perhaps you would like to look me up by calling my name and we can have many discussions about all these things at length, and I can show you they are all true.

After all, it's got to be better than forever blowing a trumpet.

Until then, I know the Creator of all life will draw you ever closer to eternal love.

Printed in Great Britain
by Amazon